KV-294-889

# The Growth of Music

## A STUDY IN MUSICAL HISTORY

# The Growth of Music

## BY H. C. COLLES

———

**In** three parts and complete
in one volume

# The Growth of Music

## A STUDY IN MUSICAL HISTORY

### By H. C. COLLES

PART I

*From the Troubadours to J. S. Bach*

THIRD EDITION
REVISED BY ERIC BLOM

LONDON
OXFORD UNIVERSITY PRESS
*New York   Toronto*

*Oxford University Press, Ely House, London W. 1*

GLASGOW NEW YORK TORONTO MELBOURNE WELLINGTON
CAPE TOWN SALISBURY IBADAN NAIROBI LUSAKA ADDIS ABABA
BOMBAY CALCUTTA MADRAS KARACHI LAHORE DACCA
KUALA LUMPUR HONG KONG TOKYO

FIRST EDITION 1912
SECOND EDITION 1939
THIRD EDITION 1956
REPRINTED 1957, 1959, 1962, 1965
AND 1968

PRINTED IN GREAT BRITAIN

# Preface to the Third Edition

THIS modernized version of a work by the late Dr. H. C. Colles is, perhaps wrongly, called a 'revised edition'. One does not revise scholars like Colles. But unfortunately the work of any scholar, however excellent at its inception, has a way of going out of date; and the author of the present one, whose modesty equalled his learning, would have been the first to admit that he too would inevitably come to be judged from points of view different from his own. There is no doubt that, had he lived to produce a new edition in 1955, he would have changed his book far more radically than I ventured to take it upon myself to do. It is even possible that he would have felt the title, *The Growth of Music*, no longer suitable to whatever revision he might have undertaken. He was brought up in a school that held to a doctrine, characteristic of the later nineteenth century, according to which music had developed by a process of trial and error towards the ultimate perfection of Wagner or Brahms—according to taste. But he must sooner or later have been struck by the fact that the choice between these two was indeed a matter of taste, and suspected that if they were different from each other in kind but not necessarily in degree of eminence, they differed in the same way from Bach or Beethoven without being greater merely because they came later. What is more, if Brahms, for example, had been his chosen favourite among all the great masters, he would have had to decline seeing further moves towards perfection in Strauss or Debussy or Stravinsky, and thus perforce to abandon his view of 'growth' for one merely of 'change'. Again, if he thought metrical melody an advance on plainsong or major and minor tonality an improvement on modality, simply on chronological evidence, he would also have had to admit the twelve-note system on which so much of mid-twentieth-century music is based to be superior to that of the major and minor keys. But we may be sure that he would very much sooner have given up any notion of a continual 'improvement' in music than let Schoenberg usurp the place of Brahms in his affection.

However, what Colles might have done to his own work in the light of present-day musical taste and learning is one thing; it was quite another for me to bring his book up to date. It must remain essentially his book, and if only because it is so well known under its original title, it must also remain the *Growth of Music*. If 'growth' is understood to mean an ever-increasing expansion of ways and means rather than a progress towards some unimaginable ultimate perfection, it may still serve well enough, and I have tried to make some changes that will facilitate such understanding without attempting to interfere with the author more drastically than I like to think he would have approved of my doing. A large number of his pages I have left untouched, and I have interfered neither with his style nor with any incidental expression of opinion—as distinct from purely factual observations—to which I felt he would have wished to adhere.

It only remains for me to hope that *The Growth of Music* in its present version will not look too much like patchwork. Indeed, it was in that hope that I refrained from giving any indication of what is original and what is my responsibility, for any such device could not have failed to be worrying to the reader's eye. Since I did not attempt to match my own with Colles's very distinctive style, I fancy it will be sufficiently evident what is his and what mine; and it is, of course, open to anyone who wishes to check my share in the work to compare this edition with the second, last reprinted in 1954, on which it is based. My only desire is to perpetuate what has long been regarded as a very valuable introductory study in a form that would not have too greatly displeased its author.

ERIC BLOM

*May* 1956

# Contents

# *A Note on the Use of this Book*

MUSICAL history cannot be learned from a book. It is the uninterrupted record from the work of unknown composers in a far-away age to those of famous men who are living today. All that a book can do is to help the study of the music by pointing out what influence helped to mould the work of each master and what resources were added to the art with the birth of each masterpiece.

This book undertakes a still humbler task. So far from taking each master or masterpiece it merely makes a small selection of a few of the salient works by a few of the greatest men, and tries to trace the growth of musical technique by means of them. No apology is offered for the many omissions of even great names of men and works. The whole object has been to discuss as far as possible those works which people are likely to hear at concerts, in church, or on the radio, television, or gramophone; which they may play or hear played at home. In the first two chapters, however, it has not been possible to do this entirely, and that is why these chapters contain fuller musical quotations in the text than it has been necessary to make in the later ones. The final chapter, on the music of the twentieth century, which has been newly added to the present edition, also falls out of the general picture. Instead of singling out great composers or works, it attempts, merely for the sake of such completeness as is compatible with brevity, to give a general picture of the schools and tendencies that have made modern music what it is, with a minimum of critical judgement.

If this book is used for reading in school, teachers will find that each chapter is divided into sections, one or more of which may be made the basis of a lesson, according to the capacity of the pupils. But the one thing which the teacher must remember is that the contents of the book should always be made tributary to the music itself. Most schools nowadays have a gramophone and some sort of a record library, and this must be used as extensively as possible to illustrate and reinforce (or controvert) the argument of the book. There are notes at the end of each chapter suggesting what music can most usefully be played in this way (do not forget to make frequent breaks : listening can be an exhausting activity). But even when this is done it should be constantly borne in mind that the only real music is 'live' music. If the teacher can do so, he should persuade a pianist, or violinist, or better still an ensemble of some kind, to come and play to his pupils as often as possible, though not for long at any one time. And of course, if his pupils can themselves make music, that is so much the better.

The ordinary reader should also find the notes on suggested listening useful. He must find out for himself, however, whether, and where, records of the suggested material are available. No references to actual issues can be made here, for various reasons, the most obvious being that such references could not be relied on to remain up to date for more than a few months. Not only are new records constantly issued, but unfortunately old ones are almost as constantly withdrawn from the market. The best thing to do is thus to map out what records it is desirable to use for illustration, and then to seek the aid of a good gramophone shop or library to ascertain which of them are obtainable at any given time. Many famous or popular works are, of course, to be had several times over, performed by different artists; but the choice of the interpreters, which is not so very important where it is mainly a question of making the first acquaintance of this or that work, may safely be left to the reader's taste or opportunity.

Also included at the end of each chapter are suggestions for further reading. The books referred to naturally tend to be somewhat more technical and advanced than this one, but they should help readers to follow up points not fully dealt with here.

The plan of the book requires little explanation, but one detail, the use of the numerous cross-references which it contains, may be here explained. It is part of the scheme to show that the great men who gave us our music were not isolated phenomena, each one working out his own salvation without reference to his neighbour, but that they have all been links in a chain and mutually dependent. No one of them therefore must be studied alone. Purcell must at one point be referred back to Tallis and at another to Lully; Bach again was influenced even more widely by Italian and French music as well as by his German predecessors, and there was even a Toccata by Purcell among his manuscript copies. The influences upon Handel were equally numerous, and the farther we go the more deep seem to be the roots of the art, so that when we come to modern composers we find a whole range of historical development in their work. Nor does this in the least damage originality. Bach's French Suites are not less unmistakably Bach because the composer learnt something from the style of Couperin, nor Handel's arias less Handel because he met Alessandro Scarlatti as a young man and studied his methods. Each man added something of himself to what he found already existing, and not the greatest revolutionary in the world ever succeeded in shaking himself free and making an entirely fresh start. It is equally important to see what the great men have discarded as it is to see upon what they have built, and as the revolutionaries, of whom Monteverdi is the outstanding example in this volume, have always retained a certain vein of conservatism, so those who most held to tradition, such as Palestrina, have yet had their share of reform.

Moreover, since these men all live now in their works, it is often helpful to explain the earlier by the later. Handel is a good preparation for the study of Corelli and Bach for Palestrina (or indeed for practically anybody), and so the more modern composers are constantly repaying the debt which they owed to their predecessors at first by securing fuller appreciation for them afterwards. One finds the process going on among our concert audiences; people learn to appreciate Beethoven through the more obvious attractions of Tchaikovsky, while the love of

Puccini secures sympathy for Gluck. And so an occasional reversal of chronological order may illuminate a lesson in musical history.

These and kindred points will be best realized if in addition to reading the book in its chronological sequence the corresponding sections in the various chapters are taken together, so as to illustrate different musical strata, such as the development of church music from the medieval forms to the Protestant types of England and Germany as shown in Purcell and Bach, or that of harpsichord music (which eventually became piano music) in the work of the English Elizabethans and later Domenico Scarlatti in Italy, Couperin in France, and Bach and Handel. The number of lines which can be followed out is indeed almost inexhaustible. The sectional headings with the references, and perhaps some of the remarks under those headings, may prove helpful to this kind of study. At any rate the book is issued in that hope.

# CHAPTER I

# From the Troubadours to Monteverdi

WE take so many things for granted in our music that it is often difficult to realize how long it took musicians to discover the use of them, or that music of a different kind existed long ago, music as valuable in its way as that with which we are familiar, though without certain features that now seem indispensable to us.

The errand boy who whistles a tune as he goes from door to door makes the accents fall in with the regular tramp of his feet on the pavement, because his tune is naturally divided into a number of equal measures. We say he has a sense of **Rhythm,** and unconsciously he illustrates one of the great principles of modern music, **Time.**

The two things are not the same, for rhythm expressed to the ear in sound and to the eye by movements of the body, either marching or dancing, seems to be one of the first instincts of human beings, whereas time in the musical sense took hundreds of years to develop. In order to see the difference look at this tune by Haydn:

Ex. 1

The phrases bracketed '*a*' and '*b*' are in the same rhythm and time, though the notes are different. Beat out either of them with raps on the table and you will find that the result is the same. But the larger phrases, bracketed 'A' and 'B', are in quite different rhythms, as you will feel at once if you beat them, although they are in the same time. They take an equal time to play, and they are divided into measures, or bars, of equal length, having accents falling regularly at the beginning of each one. If a savage were so fortunate as to make up a tune in the rhythm '*a*', he would go on repeating it till he was tired of it, and then he would make up another rhythm which probably would represent a quite different time. Indeed, the power of joining many rhythms together by making them conform to one time is almost a new thing considering for how long people have loved and studied music, and a great deal of fine music has been written by composers who had little or no idea of time and who had to rely on their sense of rhythm to give shape to what they wrote. When the music was written to be danced to, the steps of the dancers would suggest the musical rhythm, and as we trace out the progress of music we shall find that dancing in particular helped tremendously in the development of musical rhythm and time.

There is another part of music which we all take for granted but which is even newer than time, namely, **Harmony**. Many people who can scarcely play the piano at all can 'vamp' an accompaniment to a song, and if you play them the tune you mean to sing they will immediately put a few simple chords to it which suggest that it belongs to a certain **Key**. Suppose the song to be the old English one, 'Early one morning'; if the accompanist is not very clever he will use some such chords as those shown at A (Ex. 2), that is, three common chords of which F, B flat, and C are the bass notes. These are chosen unconsciously because they are most representative of the key of F, since between them they use all the notes of its diatonic scale and no others. But if the accompanist were a little more clever he would give more variety to the harmony, introducing other chords with notes which are not members of the diatonic scale, as at B. Here the three main chords are the same and occur on all the accents (except in bar 6), but others are used between them where the asterisks are placed. The notes E flat and B natural do not interfere with the key, the harmonization is just as clearly in F as before, but it is richer and more varied.

Ex. 2

Many people who know nothing about harmony can make up an accompaniment of this kind at the piano. They have no idea why they choose certain chords rather than others, but they have an instinct for **Tonality**, i.e. the grouping of chords together around a key-note. These people, like the whistling boy, do quite easily what clever musicians only four hundred years ago achieved with the utmost difficulty, and what one hundred years before that they never thought of doing at all, and yet at that date very beautiful music was being written.

While we are on the subject of harmonizing tunes there is one other distinction to be made clear as to the ways in which it may be done. If you play a hymn-tune as it is written in *Hymns Ancient and Modern* you are really playing what the composer intended should be sung by four voices : treble, alto, tenor, and bass. Take, for example, 'All people that on earth do dwell' (A. & M. 166); the tune itself is written for the treble voice or right hand of the pianist, and you feel this to be the most important part of all. If you cannot play well enough to grasp all the notes you at least make sure of playing all that belong to the tune. Next in importance come the bass ones, the lowest in the left hand, and many people play hymn-tunes fairly well when they can play the notes of the treble and the bass quite correctly and merely fill in as many of the inner ones, alto and tenor, as their hands can reach conveniently. It is imperfect but quite passable because we listen most to the tune, next to the bass which makes it fairly clear what the harmonies are to be, and all that the inner parts have to do is to complete the chords which the bass suggests. If you play the alto or tenor parts alone the effect is scarcely like music at all, for they have very little tune of their own; sometimes they repeat the same note over and over again if it happens to agree well with the treble and the bass (cf. alto lines 2 and 3, tenor lines 2 and 4).

This way of writing music is called **homophonic**, which means 'like-sounding', that is to say, the voices are all made to agree with one set of sounds which is called the tune and contains the chief beauty. The other parts taken together must produce a beauty of harmony, but they may have little or no beauty of melody when taken singly.

We are so used to this style of harmony in hymn-tunes, in partsongs, and in pieces for the piano that it seems to us the simplest one, and it is hard to realize that another style which is more difficult to understand was actually perfected by composers long before they had learnt to use the homophonic one at all successfully. That style is called **polyphonic**, which means 'many-sounding', and when a piece of music is written in this way each one of the parts, treble, alto, tenor, and bass, sings a tune so that if you heard it alone you would say that it had distinct musical beauty. Of course the parts have still to agree with one another: if they do not, but sound ugly when they are put together, the result is not polyphonic but 'cacophonic', which means 'bad-sounding', just as when a brass band and a barrel-organ play different tunes in the same street. But though the several parts of polyphonic music must agree, their agreement is not the chief point, but rather their differences both of melody and rhythm.

The simplest form of polyphonic music is a 'catch' such as 'Three blind mice' in which the voices all sing different portions of the same tune at once (see 'Sumer is icumen in', p. 29). But it need not be the same tune, nor need all the parts be equally interesting at once; the only essential feature of polyphonic music is that each must have a separate existence of its own, as it were, besides what it contributes to the harmony of the whole.

### MEDIEVAL SONGS AND DANCES

If we consider that all music began with the making of tunes we see how men learnt to write polyphonic music, for in the process of finding out how their tunes might be made to fit together they discovered that certain notes sounded simultaneously make harmonious chords and others inharmonious ones. But the medieval notions of what is harmonious were not the same as ours: major thirds were not at once felt to be so, and minor thirds even less, nor were their inversions as minor and major sixths regarded as consonant.

It would be impossible to find a time when tunes of some sort were not made up and sung to poetry or used as dances, and as both poetry and dance steps suggest strong rhythm most of the early tunes were more remarkable for their rhythm than for any other feature. In the thirteenth century we find the Troubadours and Trouvères of France, the Minstrels of England, and the

Minnesinger of Germany all busily engaged in composing and
singing both tunes and poetry; and besides these there were the
songs of the people, that is to say, songs made by unknown
authors which were passed from mouth to mouth and altered
and often improved in the process, some of which have lasted to
the present day and are generally called 'folk-songs'.

There was also the music of the church which we know very
much more about, because the monasteries were the chief seats
of learning, and the monks took more trouble than the secular
musicians to find a way of writing down music accurately, so
that their work is much better preserved now, with the result
that we are apt to think that there was less, or less important,
secular music in the Middle Ages, compared with the music for
the church. We are also apt to suppose that it was church music
which contributed most to the evolution of polyphonic music,
merely because so much of it is preserved, and because it did in
the course of time take much the largest share in its advance.
The curious fact is, however, that from about the tenth to the
twelfth century it retarded rather than promoted polyphonic
writing in free parts, and on the other hand established a habit
of singing in vertical block chords and so pointed towards
homophonic music. For a custom arose of singing plainsong in
two or three parts by a device known as *organum*. This was due
in the first place simply to the different pitches of the alto, tenor,
and bass voices of the church choirs, each of which sang the
plainsong melody in the register most suited to it, but in parallel
lines, not in independent parts. It was found that the intervals
most satisfying to the medieval ear at which this could be
done were fifths if two voices were singing, and superimposed
fourths and fifths if three were engaged. Rigid block chords,
such as these, where the plainsong melody of 'Dies irae' is in the
middle part:

Ex. 3*a*

taught later composers the value of this kind of effect used as contrast against other textures, and it still survives in its primitive form in such a passage as this in Debussy's *La Cathédrale engloutie*:

Ex. 3*b*

with the only difference that the medieval fourths and fifths, which are still present, are here filled in with thirds.

The parallel progressions of the *organum* gradually began to be felt as being too stiff, and small changes were introduced which, for instance, permitted an interchange between fourths and fifths at certain points. Then thirds and sixths began to creep in occasionally, still as dissonances; but once this had begun to happen, there was no reason why composers should not experiment with more varied combinations, and thus chords of different kinds established themselves in their own right, and no longer merely as incidental clashes where polyphonic parts converged to produce contrasts of consonance and dissonance. Counterpoint and harmony met half-way, establishing the modern approach to musical composition which no longer dictated that music should be either purely polyphonic or purely homophonic, but permitted it to use freely a mixture of both these procedures according to the composer's choice.

The most important contribution to medieval music was made by France, inside the church by the great twelfth–thirteenth century Notre-Dame school, and outside by three different classes of people: (1) the quite untaught populace that cultivated folk-song; (2) the southern Troubadours, who included princes and kings such as Guillaume, Duke of Guienne, and Richard

Cœur de Lion; and (3) the northern Trouvères, among whom was Adam de La Halle.

From its earliest days French poetry has been very clear and definite in form, and French musicians took care to make the music fit the words closely, so that their tunes took character from the poetry and were written in neat little phrases finished with cadences. Moreover songs and dances often went together in France, and plays in which the characters both sang and danced soon became very popular.

Among the first of these, and the one from which we will take an example, was a pastoral play by Adam de La Halle called *Robin et Marion* which was played in 1285. Here is one of the songs in which Robin is courting the love of Marion, and he does it just as in so many English folk-songs, such as 'The Keys of Canterbury', by offering her presents. In this verse he invites her to eat a *pâté* with him; then the dialogue goes on and he asks her if she wishes for anything more. She replies most emphatically that she does, and so he sings again to the same tune offering her a 'capon' (*chapon*). It is all very artless, but what we have to notice is the perfect neatness and crispness of the tune, partly suggested by the lines of verse and partly by the need of carrying on a rhythm to which the actors could dance:

Ex. 4

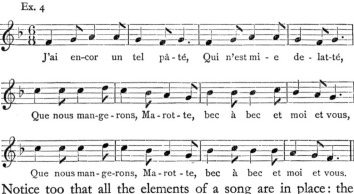

J'ai  en-cor  un  tel  pâ-té,  Qui n'est mi-e  de-lat-té,

Que nous man-ge-rons, Ma-rot-te, bec  à  bec  et moi et vous,

Que nous man-ge-rons, Ma-rot-te, bec  à  bec  et moi  et vous.

Notice too that all the elements of a song are in place: the first phrase repeated to give balance, then another ('Que nous mangerons') carried on in the way called a 'sequence', that is by repeating it on other notes ('bec à bec'), and then the refrain made out of the repetition of the words and tune with a cadence added. The whole is so perfect and suggests to our ears such simple harmony that it is hard to believe that it was written without thought of harmony, or that, if Adam de La Halle did think of harmony, it would have been unlike what we imagine. When he and his contemporaries wrote music for two or three voices to sing in harmony they brought chords together which seem to us most incongruous, because as we have already seen in the case of *organum* they merely calculated what intervals would go well with each note of the tune and did not think of the result in chords at all. Their ideas of what would go well, moreover, were very different from ours, since they regarded fifths, fourths, and octaves as the most consonant intervals. In our first harmony lessons we are taught to avoid these because of their bareness; we have learnt that thirds and sixths are sweeter, and if you try to 'sing seconds' to a tune you generally follow it in a series of thirds below, thus:

Ex. 5

Major,     Minor,     Minor, Major, &c.

using a major or a minor third according to which fits in best with the scale, in this instance G. But the old writers would not have agreed with you. They would have added their harmonies probably above the tune, consisting of fifths and fourths, and they would have used only perfect intervals, not taking any account of the notes of the key as we do. It was only gradually that a taste grew for other intervals, and a desire for each separate chord to be harmonious. It was a long time before what we now know as the triad and the chord of the sixth became acceptable. All the process of making harmonized music, therefore, began by adding parts or tunes to one which had been already composed without regard to effects of harmony, but rather as something which might be sung quite by itself.

### CHURCH MUSIC

What men like Adam de La Halle began to do in the way of supplying songs with harmony, monks and churchmen did much more consistently, so that for nearly three hundred years the main development of polyphonic music was carried on by these faithful workers whose business it was to supply the daily offices of the church with music.

The tunes which they first had to work upon were the old 'plainsong' melodies which had been handed down traditionally and sometimes altered and improved upon by the singers in churches much in the same way that the folk-songs were being treated by the people, so that these melodies became the basis of church music just as folk-song became the basis of secular song.

But the two kinds of melody were not long kept distinct. It is often difficult to tell whether an old song originally belonged to the church or the world, for the musicians of each borrowed from one another. Tunes which the people heard in church would be used for secular words and turned into popular songs, while the monks often deliberately adopted popular tunes, and, so to speak, wrote their masses round them. Here is a very famous French folk-song called *L'homme armé* ('The man at arms') which was taken as the basis or, as it was called, the *canto fermo* (fixed song) of a great many masses written by the Flemish composers of the fifteenth century:

Ex. 6

L'hom - me, l'hom - me, l'homm' ar · mé,     L'homm' ar -

FINE.

- mé doibt   on dou - ter.     On   a   fait   par

tout  cri - er    Que  chas - cun    se  viengu' ar -

- mer  D'un  hau - bre - gon  de    fer. . . . .    D.C.

Notice that the tune itself has very strong rhythm and a clear form. Though the first part is never exactly reproduced in the sequel, the downward phrases are copied to some extent and are really the same phrase written on different parts of the scale. If it were a modern tune we should say that it modulates into the key of G and then returns to that of C major; but that is not precisely the case, for according to the principles of what was called *musica ficta* it was left to the singer to put in the F sharp or not, and it is now uncertain how far it was a question of taste or a matter of unwritten rules to make these changes at sight. But be that as it may, musicians never thought of a change of pitch as meaning a change of key. Still, the placing of the same phrase in different positions shows that the unknown composer had a strong feeling for contrast of pitch.

What composers did was to take this tune instead of the plainsong of the mass and set one voice to sing the sacred words to it while the others sang the words to free and flowing melodies which were quite independent. Ex. 7 is a short extract from a 'Sanctus' by JOSQUIN DES PRÉS (born *c.* 1450), one of the distinguished composers of the Netherlands, who carried the art to Italy when he, like many of his countrymen, went to Rome and became a member of the papal choir.

You see that the tune is buried among the other parts. It is not set at all as though it were the most important thing to be heard, as we should set it; it is put into very long notes so that its merry rhythm is lost, and this was done partly that it might have

Ex. 7

some of the solemn dignity fit for church music, and partly in
order that the other voices, which take no account of it except
to agree with it in consonant intervals at the principal accents,
might move the more freely. There is something incongruous
between the tune (or *canto fermo*) and its counterpoints (i.e.
notes or 'points' written against it); the tune would be more
expressive without the elaborate counterpoints, and the counterpoints would be more beautiful without these stiff-sounding
long notes held on amongst them. Nevertheless, though this
way of composing seems clumsy to us, Josquin was a very great
composer who wrote most beautiful-sounding passages for the
voices.

Two things, however, which we consider essential to music
are quite absent from this and from most of the church music of

† The part is sung an octave lower than it is written.

the fifteenth century; they are **rhythm** and **key**, which we saw at the outset are now felt instinctively by every one who is at all musical. The early folk-songs and troubadour songs show that the old musicians had the feeling for rhythm equally with our-selves, but in seeking out the art of writing counterpoint the church musicians lost sight of rhythm to a considerable extent. It was natural enough, for the very conditions of their work took it away from the influences of dancing and poetry and it became more and more contemplative and less spontaneous.

The feeling for key on the other hand had never been reached, and could not be reached until chords and their relations to one another were more fully understood. A modern musician would consider the first phrase of *L'homme armé* as used by Josquin to be in the key of B flat, or possibly F, and either view would shut out the chord of E minor (marked *); but Josquin merely considered that the tune was written on a certain series of notes called the **mode**, and that any notes which were consonant with these and with each other could be made effective. He had no conception of what we call the **tonic chord** as a centre and other chords supporting it and contrasting with it as the domi-nant and subdominant do in Ex. 2.

A definite feeling of key is bound up with the modern major and minor scales, and chromatic alterations are permitted within these by the use of accidentals to a much larger extent than *musica ficta* allowed. These alterations in turn can effect modulation from key to key (thus F sharp in the key of C major turns it towards G major and B flat towards F major), whereas there was no such thing as modulation from mode to mode. But although the modes did not permit modulation, which is one of the great resources of the key system, it must not be thought that they were inferior makeshifts for something that was eventually to bring about a great improvement. As the predecessors of tonality they have their own perfection and obey laws as valid artistically as those which govern the major and minor keys. The old church modes have their roots as far back as ancient Greek music—hence their Greek names, which

are, however, differently applied to the various modes—and
the four authentic modes (let us disregard the plagal ones which
merely have their final tonic on a different degree of the scale)
are as follows, if played on the white keys of the piano:

> D—D   Dorian mode,
> E—E   Phrygian mode,
> F—F   Lydian mode,
> G—G   Mixolydian mode.

To these were added in the sixteenth century:

> A—A   Aeolian mode,
> C—C   Ionian mode.

The last is identical with our major scale; the Aeolian with
our minor scale in its descending form.

The work of Josquin and the others of his time strikes modern
ears—but modern ears only—as though a great deal of beautiful
material were in need of sorting out and arranging in a more
definite order than the composers themselves understood. A
gradual process of achieving orderliness in a way that comes
nearer to the procedures to which the 'classical' era of music has
accustomed us was undergone by music in the hands of composers of the fifteenth and sixteenth centuries.

### THE MADRIGAL

Though one can trace this process in their church music, it was
even more strongly forwarded in their settings of secular words
to be sung by several voices in the polyphonic style which were
called **Madrigals**.

Again we find the influence of poetry exerted to recall musicians to the fact that rhythm is the true basis of their art, and
that however attractive the sound of many voices singing many
melodies may be they must conform to some common standard
of rhythm in order to produce an effect of unity. Such men as
WILLAERT and ARCADELT, who, like Josquin, were northerners,
but who lived in Italy (both were masters of the choir of

St. Mark's in Venice), wrote both church music and madrigals, but the latter are the more famous. In their madrigals the counterpoints became simpler, and in the best of them the length of the musical phrase was regulated by the length and accents of the poetic lines. Often a single note was used to each syllable as in the old songs, or if more were used for the sake of expression, they were grouped together into a clear phrase instead of wandering vaguely and holding on a single syllable until the words and sense became unrecognizable.

In their work and in that of ORLANDE DE LASSUS (1532–94), the last and greatest of the northern school, the music became divided into phrases by distinct and beautiful **cadences**, which have the same effect in music as good punctuation has in literature. If the stops are left out or badly distributed in a book even the wisest words become nonsense, for there is nothing to show where one idea ends and another begins, and similarly the division of musical sentences is shown by the use of certain chords which make an ending and separate one idea from another, and these are called cadences.

Ex. 8

Le faux A - mour d'arc et de flèches s'arme, et
prend .... son feu pour me li - vrer l'as - saut.
et prend
prend son feu pour me .... li - vrer l'as - saut.

This opening of a graceful little French song for four voices by
Lassus shows how closely he could make his music follow the
metre of words. Notice the cadences (marked †) at the ends of
the lines, and also the fact that although the counterpoint is
very simple each voice moves quite freely at the words 'et
prend' without destroying the rhythm of the verse.

Both in his madrigal and in his church works (Masses,
Magnificats, and the famous settings of the Penitential Psalms)
Lassus used the same means for giving order and clearness to
his ideas, but in his church music he was not so closely bound
by the rhythm of words as he was in setting secular poetry.
Where, as in the Penitential Psalms, he had great and deep feelings to express, he naturally thought more of beauty of melody
and of making the voices join in rich and varied harmony, but
even in these the rhythmic form is not disregarded as it was in
the church music written before the rise of the madrigal.


### PALESTRINA

The man who put the crown on the whole method of polyphonic writing for voices was an Italian, GIOVANNI PIERLUIGI
DA PALESTRINA. The name Palestrina is that of the small
cathedral town in the hill country near Rome where he was
born about the end of 1525. He lived most of his life in Rome,
holding appointments in the papal choir and working with untiring devotion to compose some of the loveliest and most
purely religious church music which has ever been written.

Most of the Italian church composers in the early part of the
sixteenth century had not reached anything like the simplicity
of style which the settlers from the north had acquired in their
madrigals and imported into their church music. There is a
well-known story that polyphonic music was in danger of being
banished altogether from the services of the church by the
reforms of the Council of Trent (1562) on account of its elaborateness which made the words of the liturgy unintelligible, but
that Palestrina saved it by writing some masses which were so

pure and expressed the devotional feeling of the words so aptly that the Council decided not to destroy the good with the bad. The story itself is not true to facts, but like most stories of the kind, it was based upon a certain truth, and shows where the strength of Palestrina's music lay. He began where Josquin left off, writing masses on *L'homme armé* and other *canti fermi* of a more or less mechanical kind. He soon outgrew the mechanism and found well-ordered forms for his musical thoughts inspired solely by the words which he set.

Let us take two instances from the famous *Missa Papae Marcelli* (Mass of Pope Marcellus), the work with which his reform of church music is generally associated—the beginning of the 'Kyrie eleison' (Lord have mercy) and the beginning of the 'Gloria'. In the first instance each one of the six voices sings the same beautiful fragment of melody—'Kyrie' on a long sustained note, the music rising by the interval of a 4th on the second syllable of 'eleison'. The phrases are very simple and yet exactly express the aspiration of the prayer, and the passage shows how perfectly Palestrina was able to make each voice move in an independent and gracious flow of melody, while at the same time they unite in expressing the one idea. But the beginning of the 'Gloria' is quite different. Here, instead of the voices all singing independently, they are grouped together into strong and dignified chords. The first phrases hardly seem to be polyphonic music at all, but rather homophonic, so smoothly do the parts move in harmony and rhythm. Soon, however, the independence of the voices makes itself felt in such beautiful figures as the tenor sings to the words 'laudamus Te' (We praise Thee). Each clause of the words 'We praise Thee, we bless Thee' has some such musical feature to give it distinction, but it is not till the climax is reached 'Fili unigenite, Jesu Christe' (O only begotten Son, Jesu Christ) that the voices spread out into the full splendour of the polyphonic style.

In reading Palestrina's music it is well to remember that he did not write it with bar lines as it is printed now, and so the bar lines are no indication of accent. There is rhythm in his music, but not time in the sense explained at the beginning of this chapter. Again, there is no clear notion of key, though the cadences, first on G, then on A, then on C, in this 'Gloria' show him feeling his way in that direction.

One more example of Palestrina's music will impress these points about time and key still more strongly. It is the first phrase of his exquisite setting of the Latin hymn 'Stabat Mater' which he wrote quite near to the end of his life, about 1590:

Ex. 9

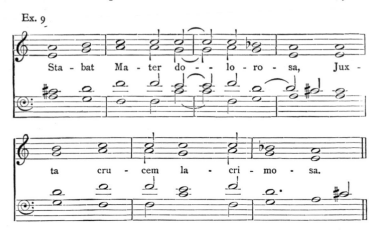

The music gives the 'quantities' of the verse exactly, but the bar lines, if they had any effect upon the rhythm, would throw out the accents of the second line. Further, the example shows that Palestrina fully understood the beauty of contrasted chords, but his use of chords of A, G, F, at the outset, and of both the major and minor form of the chord of G, proves that his chords are not connected by a key system such as ours. To understand and enjoy the music of Palestrina we have first to rid our minds of the principles of time and key which modern music has engrained, but the more familiar one is with it, the more one can realize the wonderful variety which he obtained from simple contrasts such as have been remarked.

## A REVOLUTION

Although after Palestrina's death in 1594 the same serene and beautiful style of writing for voices in church music and madrigals was carried on by composers such as Victoria, Ingegneri, and Soriano, an entirely new influence soon made its appearance which overturned the art of composition to such an extent that it seemed to be establishing just the opposite principles to those which had guided the great choral composers.

This was nothing less than the beginning of **Opera**, that is to say the performance of stage plays in which the characters sing their words to an accompaniment played by instruments instead of speaking them. It would be difficult to say quite how old the idea was. We know that songs and acting had gone together in the 'mystery' and 'miracle' plays of the Middle Ages as well as in the secular plays of the French (see p. 8). But now in the year 1594, the very year of Palestrina's death, a number of artists, both poets and musicians, assembled in the house of a nobleman of Florence, not to revive the musical plays of the Middle Ages, which they heartily despised as belonging to an age of superstitious folly, but to copy the drama of the Greeks by setting musical notes to poetry in such a way as both to express the meaning of the words and to preserve their metre and accent accurately. There was a distinct difference between their object and that of the medieval songs which often kept close to the feeling and metre of the words, because the first object of these songs was always to make a beautiful tune, whereas the Florentine experimenters did not want to write tunes at all, but only to express the words in musical notes rising and falling as the voice of a reciter would rise and fall. And so they eventually established the kind of singing which we now call **recitative**, because it reproduces the expression of a reciting voice and has no definite rhythm or tune apart from the words.

One of the earliest operas of the kind which has been preserved is a setting of the story of *Euridice* by Jacopo Peri, which was performed at Florence in 1600. The old and beautiful legend of the musician, Orpheus, who so loved his wife, Eurydice, that he brought her back from death, became at once one of the most popular subjects for opera, and other settings appeared almost immediately, notably one by Giulio Caccini, who was a singer and the writer of some beautiful songs.

But these early efforts were comparatively amateurish, and the man who really proved what tremendous possibilities this kind of music possessed was CLAUDIO MONTEVERDI (born 1567), the first of the great revolutionary composers whose stories we shall tell in studying the growth of modern music. The date shows that Monteverdi was not a very young man at the time when the Florentine musicians began their experiments in opera. He was over thirty when Peri's *Euridice* was produced, and he had been educated by his teacher, Ingegneri, in the strict tradition of the old choral music and himself wrote a number of madrigals and continued to write then after he had taken to writing operas in the new style. But his madrigals show his love of trying experiments and they contain a number of curious harmonies which make them less smoothly perfect of their kind than similar works by his predecessors.

We shall generally find that the men who discovered new ways of making music have begun by writing less fluently than others in the older styles because they could not be satisfied with what had been already done, and they could not find a new way without beginning by spoiling the old. Handel complained that Gluck knew no more of counterpoint than his cook, Waltz; Mendelssohn shook his head over technical blunders in Wagner's *Tannhäuser*; and fifty years ago people blamed Richard Strauss because some of the sounds which his orchestra makes are crude in comparison with Wagner's orchestra. They are all right in one sense, but people only make great discoveries by risking a good deal, and that is the way in which music grows.

The first of Monteverdi's operas which has been preserved and the most celebrated of all his works is *Orfeo*, a setting of the same story as Peri's *Euridice*, though called by the name of the hero instead of by that of the heroine. It was produced at the court of the Duke of Mantua in 1607, for at that time there were no such things as public opera houses, and works of the kind could only be performed for the pleasure of rich people who chose to pay for the entertainment. The one and only rule which Monteverdi followed in writing *Orfeo* was the determination to make every part of his music express the feelings which the words of the play described.

### THE ORCHESTRA

In the first place, since the voices sang separately he had to form an orchestra to accompany them, but he was not content with just a few instruments to support the voices; he needed them to take part in the descriptive effects of the opera, and so he gathered together practically all the kinds of instruments then existing in order to have the advantages of their different sorts of tone.

Organs had been in use in churches for some time, and besides the big ones which were fixed in their places, small chamber organs, which were something like small harmoniums, were in use. Monteverdi decided to have two of these in his orchestra. Then there were instruments rather like a grand piano in shape, but in which the strings were plucked by a quill instead of being struck by a hammer; they were called by the Italians *gravicembalo*, our name for them is 'harpsichord'. Lutes of various sizes, the strings of which were plucked by the fingers as in the modern guitar, and the harp had been used to accompany voices in songs, and Monteverdi included all these.

No instrument in which the strings are plucked makes a very sonorous effect, because however sharply the plucking is done the tone stops at once, just as when the violin is played *pizzicato* (that is, with the fingers). Although these instruments seem a pretty large force, and most of them were so bulky that they must have taken up a great deal of space, the actual musical result from them would be so small that we should probably think it weak in comparison with one modern piano.

But Monteverdi was not content with only these. He also required twelve instruments of the violin family in various sizes, 'two little violins of the French kind', three bass viols, two recorders, some trumpets, two *cornetti* (wind intruments made of wood with a trumpet mouthpiece), and five trombones.

If he had set these to play all at once he would have had a fairly powerful orchestra, but as a matter of fact the wind instruments and even the strings were not allowed to be heard constantly with the voices, and some of the wind instruments were so imperfect that they could only play a few notes. The piece of music for orchestra which begins the opera, called 'Toccata', is merely a sort of 'fanfare' on a single chord of C, evidently so written in order that the trumpets which, like the modern military bugle, could only play the notes of the common chord, might take part in the opening whatever happened afterwards. It is followed by a quiet passage for strings in five parts which reminds one very much of madrigal music, for the parts move in the same smooth way which is natural to voices. All through the early music for viols and violins we find passages which recall the old choral music, for musicians had to discover the scales, arpeggios, and other special kinds of figure which sound so well on stringed instruments but which voices cannot sing. Nowadays we can often tell by glancing at a piece of music what instrument it is meant for, but at the beginning of the seventeenth century not only was this impossible, but it is often difficult to tell whether a given piece was intended to be sung or played. Monteverdi scarcely wrote any notes even for the 'little violins' which a high soprano voice could not sing easily, but nevertheless some of the things which he made the players do must have seemed amazing to people whose ears were accustomed to pure choral music. For example, the effect got by drawing the violin bow rapidly to and fro on a single note thus :

Ex. 10

Written.          Played.

was a thing which Monteverdi found out and which is quite
impossible on any instrument but one played with a bow. Even
now that we are all quite used to it it has an exciting effect when
a large mass of violins tremble in this way. Imagine how impressive it must have been to unaccustomed ears, and this was
only one new effect among innumerable other ones which
Monteverdi gained from his orchestra. He was not the first to
make an orchestra. Some of his contemporaries, notably Andrea
and Giovanni Gabrieli, uncle and nephew at Venice, were at
this time writing independent pieces for groups of instruments,
strings and wind, which may be called the remote ancestors of
that kind of orchestral music which we call 'symphony'.

In his later operas, which were written to be performed
publicly at Venice, Monteverdi used a much simpler method of
instrumentation, with fewer instruments than those of *Orfeo*.
This was partly due to what he had learnt from the Venetian
composers and partly a practical economy (cf. Scarlatti, p. 56).

### THE VOICES

Let us turn now to the vocal side of the music. Here is a passage
which shows at once how different his method was from that of
the polyphonic writers. The main story of the opera is that
Eurydice dies and Orpheus mourns for her so passionately that
at last he determines to go and seek for her among the dead and
by his love and his music to draw her back to life. A shepherd
asks him for whom he weeps in this beautiful phrase:

Ex. 11

Ma tu, gen-til can-tor, s'a' tuoi   la-men - ti   già fe -

The voice is not singing a melody with any shape or rhythm of its own, it merely rises and falls with the syllables of the words, accentuating them as perfectly as possible, and their expression is reinforced by the harmonies. For example, in the third bar the words 'festi lagrimar' ('madest weep') lead him to use grinding discordant harmonies (chords of the seventh following one another chromatically) to convey the poignancy of grief. To the ears of people used to the smooth common chords of the madrigals they must have sounded more violent than any of the strange chords with which modern composers startle us.

The scene in which Orpheus visits the lower regions and demands that Eurydice shall be restored to life is another marvellous piece of writing of a quite different kind. Monteverdi was here determined to produce something weird, strange, and unearthly, and he did it by writing wild scale passages for the viols, *cornetti*, and harps, and making the singer (Orpheus) vie with them by singing all sorts of tortuous runs and turns, such as this for example:

Ex. 12

and a good deal more all on a single syllable.

Such a musical effect was of course a direct contradiction of the principle laid down by the Florentines that the words should be strictly preserved; it distorted them as much as the old church music of Josquin and others had done, and it did so for the very same reason, namely, in order to make the music more telling. These passages were in fact given the name of 'coloratura' because they were supposed to give colour to the situation. Monteverdi, of course, used them for that purpose, but they soon became very popular for their own sakes both with the singers and with the people who heard them. Singers liked to show off how cleverly they could execute the runs and shakes and other ornaments, and audiences thought them very wonderful and applauded the performance without stopping to think whether it was at all appropriate. Composers of operas soon discovered that they had a great many things to take into account besides the purely artistic effect of their works, for they had to satisfy the vanity of singers by giving them music which would show off their voices, and they had to amuse the grand people who were looking on by giving them scenes which made a great effect, and so it has happened that showy 'coloratura', fine scenery, and gorgeous dresses have often made an opera successful when both the play and the music set to it were very poor and had nothing to do with each other.

Monteverdi, however, was much too good a musician to give in to such nonsense, and like Gluck and Wagner in later ages he spent endless trouble in trying to make his music dramatic and appropriate at all points.

As far as the voices were concerned his chief means were (1) the simple recitative which the Florentines had invented, (2) beautiful fragments of melody growing out of the recitative to give effect to the more expressive words, and (3) 'coloratura' for special effects, such as the scene in the infernal regions and the one at the end of the opera, where Apollo and Orpheus ascend to heaven.

*Orfeo*, then, shows the beginning of many different kinds of music since in it there are at least three distinct kinds of solo song besides dramatic choruses and a great deal of instrumental music. The modern orchestra had its birth as it were in this opera. While Monteverdi was far from being the first composer of opera, he was the first who so combined the resources of voices and instruments in such a way as to make of opera a great form of art.

The new way of writing for a single voice with instrumental accompaniment had another very important effect: it brought about much clearer ideas of harmony. For when one voice sang alone it naturally became the most important part, and the instruments had rather to agree with it than to play independent music on their own account. Their parts became grouped together in chords which supported the voice exactly in the homophonic style which we explained early in the chapter as that of the hymn-tune.

Moreover, the frequent use of these chords, especially those of the tonic, dominant, and subdominant (cf. Ex. 2) which came so often to form the cadences helped to establish their relations to one another in a **key**. When once the existence of the key was recognized all the wonderful effects got by changing from one key to another and contrasting passages in different keys could be gradually discovered, as in fact they soon were by the composers of the next generation.

All this was not done by Italian opera alone, though it was without doubt the strongest influence at the beginning of the seventeenth century. Songs for single voice with an accompaniment for the lute or harpsichord were written by various composers, foremost among them Caccini (see p. 20), who in the year 1600 brought out a volume of them which he actually called by the name of 'The New Music'. Everywhere, too, instruments were soon more freely used. In the private houses of wealthy people both in Italy and France music for instruments alone (viols, harpsichords, and lutes) was cultivated and cantatas for a single voice accompanied by one or more instruments became popular. In those parts of Germany where the Protestant reformation had turned the old music out of the churches the use of organs to accompany the simple hymn-tunes had much the same effect in helping to establish a clear system of harmony (see p. 85).

The new music did not make itself felt so soon in England, and before going farther in tracing its course we must go back and see what had actually taken place in our own country.

## Suggestions for Further Reading and Listening

SUPPLEMENTARY reading is bound to be rather taxing in the case of this chapter, which covers many recondite subjects as well as a very long period. There are no reliable easy and popular books on early music, but useful information will be found in a comparatively small space in Robert Stevenson's *Music before the Classic Era*. For sustained study one must recommend vols. ii–iv of *The New Oxford History of Music*, which cover roughly the period dealt with in this chapter ('Early Medieval Music up to 1300', 'Ars Nova and the Renaissance', and 'The Age of Humanism') and Gustave Reese's *Music in the Middle Ages* and *Music in the Renaissance*. These are large-scale works of serious scholarship covering a number of subjects not included here. Several of the large articles in Grove's *Dictionary of Music and Musicians* may also be read with profit, especially Professor J. A. Westrup's contribution to that on Song, on the troubadours and similar secular singers, Dr. W. L. Smoldon's on the Liturgical Music-Drama (the first approaches towards opera), and Professor E. J. Dent's on the Madrigal. For those who wish to read books on the two greatest composers in this chapter there are those on Palestrina by Henry Coates ('Master Musicians' series) and on Monteverdi by Hans Redlich.

Valuable gramophone records of early music will be found in the collection entitled *Anthologie sonore*, edited by Curt Sachs and published in Paris. The most easily accessible records, however, any or all of which will offer admirable material, are those issued in connexion with the *New Oxford History of Music* under the title of *The*

*History of Music in Sound*, accompanied by a series of booklets bearing the same name which contain very full annotations of each record. The parts relevant to this chapter, like those of the *History* itself, are vols. ii–iv. Other records of works by Josquin des Prés, Arcadelt, Lassus, Palestrina, Caccini, and Monteverdi can be used to supplement the foregoing. Enterprising readers, needless to say, will not necessarily confine themselves to the few masters chosen for discussion by the author, but will wish to hear other music of the period on which they can lay their hands; and this applies not merely to the present chapter, but to the whole course outlined in this book.

# CHAPTER II

# Music in England up to the Beginning of the Seventeenth Century

So far we have left England out of count, not because its music was unimportant but because it is so important for us that it is necessary to study it in a separate chapter.

We have seen that most of the work of discovering how voices could be combined in choral music was done by composers who sprang from the northern provinces of Europe, who carried their achievements into other countries, Italy in particular. But at an earlier date it seemed almost as if this would be done by English composers. In the Middle Ages the English were great makers of ballads and songs, especially of the kind which, like the famous Agincourt Song, celebrated victories and gave voice to patriotic sentiment. Moreover, one example of early English polyphonic music survives which is such a marvellously perfect thing that it still remains a mystery how it could possibly have been written at so early a date, about the year 1240, that is to say about the time that Adam de La Halle was born. It is the famous 'round' called 'Sumer is icumen in'. Four treble (or tenor) voices sing the delightful, lilting melody in succession, just as in a modern 'round' or 'catch', and two bass voices maintain a constant refrain of 'Sing cuc-cu', making beautifully pure and rich harmony with the melodic parts. Since it was possible to make voices sing together so perfectly in the thirteenth century it is strange that progress later should have been so slow.

One composer, JOHN DUNSTABLE (born about 1390), stands out as a person of special importance, for he was contemporary with the early Netherland composers, a full generation before Josquin des Prés (see p. 11), and he was evidently quite famous all over the Continent. In 1437 one Martin Le Franc wrote a poem in French in which he compared Dunstable favourably with the only other two great composers of the time, both of them Flemings, Gilles Binchois and Guillaume Dufay, who were about ten years younger than he. He wrote, chiefly for three voices, both church music and secular songs, and from the collected edition in vol. viii of *Musica Britannica* it is easy to see that it must have been his skill in making the voices move smoothly without producing harsh harmonies which earned him his reputation.

Musicians in other countries certainly looked up to him as a leader, and that fact in itself is remarkable because between his time and the present English composers were distinctly lacking in the power of initiative. Most of their best work has been done when the way has been pointed out by others. There have been no great pioneer musicians, like Monteverdi, for example, who led the way to new and unexpected kinds of music which influenced the art of the whole world.

### CHURCH MUSIC (FIFTEENTH AND SIXTEENTH CENTURIES)

We get an immediate example of this in the fact that, though church music was cultivated seriously in England from the time that Henry VII ascended the throne (1485) after the Wars of the Roses, nothing of much practical importance to us now was accomplished until the work of the Netherlandish composers had become known to musicians in this country in the reign of Henry VIII. As soon as they were shown the way a splendid group of Englishmen came forward, and wrote masses, motets, and other service music which rival the best done elsewhere.

The first of these men was CHRISTOPHER TYE (born about 1500), who was brought up as a chorister in the choir of King's College, Cambridge, and was afterwards organist of Ely Cathedral as well as holding a place in the Chapel Royal of both Henry VIII and Edward VI.

The part that the Chapel Royal has played in the history of music in England is very important, for most of the best composers up to the end of the seventeenth century held the appointment of 'gentleman' of the choir, which meant that while they were engaged as singers they were able to devote time to composing music which was sure to be sung by the choir. They had every inducement to do good work and every chance of judging of the result when it was done, and that is the best encouragement a musician can have.

One of Tye's early works was a Mass for four voices which was written round an old English folk-song *Westron Wynde*, just as the Netherlanders used to write church music with their popular songs as a *canto fermo* (see p. 10). Though in this instance Tye copied a bad principle from his teachers, he learnt all that was good in their manner of writing. His great work was a Mass for six voices called by the name *Euge bone* (probably an allusion to an antiphon on the text 'Well done, good and faithful servant') and it is splendidly written on simple and stately themes for the most part composed for the words to which they are set, as were Palestrina's melodies in the *Missa Papae Marcelli*. The themes are often repeated and closely imitated by all the voices in turn, so that the whole effect is as strong and clear as it can be. The only fault is that it is so strictly written that it is apt to sound rather stiff. There is not the grace and freedom of melody which one finds in Lassus or Palestrina or indeed in some of the best works of the Englishmen who followed Tye. It is possible that this Mass was the one which Tye was required to compose when he took his degree of Doctor of Music at Cambridge in 1545, and this would account for its strictness. Tye and his companions wrote music which expressed deeper religious feeling and showed a finer sense of musical beauty than this Mass, though nothing could surpass its technical skill.

One of the greatest of these was THOMAS TAVERNER, organist of Cardinal Wolsey's College (now Christ Church) at Oxford, who wrote half a dozen fine settings of the Mass including one on the *Westron Wynde* tune. Another was ROBERT WHYTE, a pupil of Tye, whose daughter he married. But far more famous is THOMAS TALLIS, most distinguished of all the members of Henry VIII's Chapel Royal.

What remains of Whyte's work is so fine and like Tye's in style that one cannot help suspecting that there was more of it which has been lost. But the large quantity of Tallis's music shows that he was one of those great minds which gain more power the more they use it. It is possible to trace his growing strength through a long series of works from an early Magnificat and a Mass for four voices, in which he seems to be feeling his way as the earlier polyphonic composers did, to the beautiful series of Sacramental Motets of which *O sacrum Convivium* is the most celebrated. Both he and Whyte composed settings of the Lamentations of Jeremiah which were part of the service of 'Tenebrae' sung in Holy Week, and both are full of the tender and plaintive feeling of the words which Lassus caught so perfectly in his Penitential Psalms.

### THE REFORMATION

While all these men were still young the personal quarrels between Henry VIII and the Pope were fermenting, and none of them had gone far in their careers when it became clear that the quarrel was not to remain a personal one between King and Pope, but that it would produce drastic changes in the church in this country, though no one could tell how drastic those changes would be. The first which really affected the musicians seriously was the suppression of the greater monasteries (1539–40). This event deprived Tallis of his place as organist of Waltham Abbey, and besides merely individual losses of the kind did away at one stroke with nearly all the centres at which music had been most faithfully cultivated for generations. In fact it amounted to the destruction of the principal musical colleges of the country. Still the musicians were undaunted. The King was a friend to music; he was a performer and possibly a composer himself, though the music ascribed to him may have been revised, finished, or even written altogether by his court musicians; his chapel was maintained as fully as before, and Tallis soon found a place in it which he held through the three reigns that followed until his own death in 1585. The cathedral services too remained unchanged, and Tye continued his work at Ely without check.

But no sooner was Henry dead and his young son Edward VI on the throne than matters began to press more hardly on the church musicians. The issue of the First English Prayer Book in 1549 must have caused consternation to composers. All their lives had been occupied in setting Latin words to music, and now English was to take its place. Their work must be lost altogether except in so far as they could adapt it to the new language. They were fortunate indeed that the new Prayer Book did not for the most part introduce new services but was rather a translation of the old liturgy considerably simplified.

It is wonderful how close the English translation of the words of the Mass keeps to the sense and to the rhythm of the Latin, but the differences in the two languages offered many problems for musicians. The great difficulty lay in the number of little words (particles 'a', 'an', and 'the', which do not exist in Latin, as well as the greater quantity of prepositions in English) which are so troublesome to set to music in a dignified way worthy of the traditions of church music. Take the example of the 'Gloria' in the Mass:

'Gloria in excelsis Deo,'
*'Glory be to God on high,'*
'et in terra pax hominibus bonae voluntatis.'
*'and in earth peace goodwill towards men.'*

In the first clause the Latin requires only one preposition, the English two and the verb 'be'; the second makes use of the clumsy word 'towards'.

This is sufficient to show that the process of making music

already written suitable to the new conditions was an exceedingly difficult one, and the fact that it was done, and well done in so many cases, is in itself a proof of the genius of the sixteenth-century composers. No sooner was the First Prayer Book authorized for use than a remarkable man, JOHN MARBECK (or Merbecke), set to work to adapt the ancient plainsong to the English words, and he published his 'Booke of Common Praier Noted' (i.e. set to notes) in the following year (1550). At the present day arrangements of the Te Deum and Communion Office called by his name are often heard in churches, but they are rarely given as he wrote them. For he added no harmony to his melody, old or new; his only care was to adapt it so as to show that the traditional music could still be made use of, and he certainly proved his point.

Had the change of language been the only way in which the reformation of Edward VI affected musicians they might very soon have suited themselves to its needs and gone on writing anthems instead of motets, Communion Offices instead of Masses, in the style to which they were accustomed. But this was not all. Protestants clamoured for a simpler kind of worship altogether. For them the music like the ritual was too elaborate, because it required trained musicians for its performance. They longed to sweep it away as the Lutherans in Germany had done (see pp. 27 and 85) and to put hymns and psalms in its place in which the congregation could take part. Each one of the musicians we have been discussing met this demand in a characteristic way.

Marbeck showed once for all that the old plainsong music at least was worth preserving since it consisted solely of melody which could be learnt and sung by the people, and having done so he made no further practical contribution to the question but gave up his time to preaching and writing violent pamphlets against the Pope. He therefore drops out of musical history.

Tye, like Marbeck, sympathized with the Protestants on religious grounds, and he set himself to try to satisfy the desire for a popular form of sacred music by making a very curious experiment. He made a rhymed version of the first fourteen chapters of The Acts of the Apostles in such a way that each verse of the text became a four-lined stanza of poetry. Then he wrote a simple piece of music for each chapter which he called a motet, thus keeping the old name. Each motet was long enough to cover two of the stanzas and was to be repeated like a hymn-tune to the remaining stanzas of the chapter. Ex. 13 is part of the one to the third chapter.

Not only is it very like the homophonic hymn-tune style,

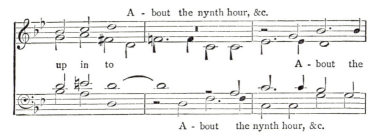

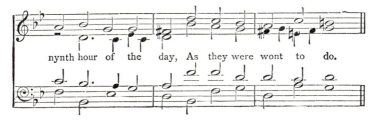

but in later years a popular hymn-tune, *Windsor*, was in fact arranged from this motet (cf. Hymns A. & M., 43). At the time when Tye made this attempt he was in a position of some influence at court. It is generally supposed that he was music master to the young King, Edward VI, and he offered his Acts of the Apostles to the King with a dedication. But they do not seem to have become very popular, probably because they were a compromise between two styles. The second stave of the example shows the voices separating into independent melodies in something like the old polyphonic style, and this occurs so often that though the motets are comparatively simple, they still needed a trained choir such as that of the Chapel Royal for their performance, so that they did not start the congregational kind of church music in England which came in a generation later when the Psalms were similarly put into verse and sung to tunes. Tye in fact after one honest effort failed to establish a Protestant form of church music, and later in the reign of Elizabeth he gave up music altogether and became a clergyman.

With Tallis the case was quite different. His own principles underwent no change; he went on writing as he had begun, only influenced to a limited extent by the outcry for simple music. He wrote an English 'Service' in D minor in which the voices all move together in plain chords instead of in separate lines of melody so that the words might be more distinctly heard than was possible in the old style, and this way of writing started what is known now as the 'Cathedral Service', which is quite as unlike popular congregational music as is the older style.

Incidentally, however, this shows us that the Protestant movement in England helped to establish the idea of harmony as consisting of series of chords as the operatic and instrumental movements in Italy did, though it worked with a very different object. Underlying both, however, was the same wish to make music conform more closely to the words (see pp. 19 and 24).

Nevertheless it soon became clear that the Protestants were

not to have it all their own way as they had in many parts of Germany. In the short reign of Mary the pendulum swung back in the direction of Roman Catholicism, and though the bigotry of the Queen and her ministers produced a distaste for Romanism from which the country has never recovered, yet after her death, when a settlement was made under Elizabeth I, Englishmen still resisted the extreme views of the strict Protestants. The outlines of public worship were preserved much as they had been determined in the Second Prayer Book of Edward VI, the cathedral foundations were maintained, and Elizabeth certainly desired that her Chapel Royal, as far as the music was concerned, should be continued with as much importance as it had had under her father. Everything was to be sung in English, but there was no check upon the elaborateness of the music. Motets by Tallis were translated into English anthems, and anthems new and old by Tallis, Whyte, and Tye written in the polyphonic manner were welcomed. Church music had weathered the storm raised against it and its future seemed bright. Yet it had suffered sorely. Tye and Marbeck had, as we saw, abandoned it for other things; Tallis's sympathies were too strongly with the Latin ritual for him to take kindly to the English one, though he remained a 'gentleman' of the choir and still wrote for it.

Curiously enough the same is true of another and a younger man, WILLIAM BYRD (1543–1623), although he was quite a little boy in the days of the First Prayer Book of Edward, and was only about sixteen years old when Elizabeth came to the throne. He, therefore, was not brought up like Tallis in the older tradition, but still he clung to it devotedly. He wrote Masses for three, four, and five voices, and many beautiful motets published under the titles *Cantiones Sacrae* and *Gradualia*, partly in conjunction with Tallis, for the Latin liturgy. For the English he composed the Great Service, as majestic in style as anything in his Latin music, and many beautiful anthems. In his short services, however, he accepted the simpler methods initiated by Tallis. A passage from an English service and a corresponding

one from the Latin Mass (five voices) will show this at a glance.
It is the opening of the 'Sanctus':

Ex. 14

Simplicity is the only advantage which the English has; the expressive beauty of the long slurred notes on the word 'sanctus' could not be reached in any kind of music which required the voices to keep to the same movement.

With Byrd, it may be said, Catholic church music reached its apex in England and at the same time Anglican music made a beginning the majesty of which it was never quite to match in later ages, though several of the Tudor composers came near it. For Byrd is at once one of the three or four supremely great English composers and one of the great masters of his time regardless of nationality, the equal of Palestrina in Italy and Victoria in Spain.

### THE MADRIGAL IN ENGLAND

The name of Byrd brings us to another instance of the way in which foreign music suggested a new outlet to our composers. In the year 1588, that in which the Spanish Armada was defeated, a certain Nicholas Yonge published a collection of Italian madrigals with the words translated into English under the title *Musica Transalpina* ('Music from across the Alps'). Previously madrigals had been known in England only through manuscript copies brought privately from abroad, and a few attempts of native composers to write in the same style, such as the well-known partsong 'In going to my naked bed' ascribed to Richard Edwards. From this time onward every composer of repute turned his attention to writing them. They were freely published and sung everywhere; so great was their popularity that the singing of madrigals became an accepted part of social intercourse, and an educated gentleman or lady would take part in a madrigal then as readily as most young people today can join in a game of tennis.

Consequently we have a host of exquisite works in which all the skill composers had gained in writing polyphonic church music was turned to account to illustrate secular poetry. No time was so rich in poetry as the reign of Elizabeth I. It was poured out in abundance by poets great and small, from geniuses such as Shakespeare and Spenser, from courtly versifiers such as Sir Philip Sidney, and from the lesser men whose verses might have been lost or forgotten if composers had not given them life by wedding them to beautiful and lasting music. This poetry had a strong effect upon musicians, wearied as they were by the endless quarrels and restrictions which had gathered round church art. It set them free again to follow their fancy, to see how music could heighten the fancy of the poet and enforce his meaning, and in doing so they learnt to use the voices more lightly, to introduce greater varieties of rhythm suggested by the language and the poetic metres.

Some of the earlier madrigals of Byrd, who published a collection called *Psalms, Sonnets and Songs of Sadness and Piety* in the same year as *Musica Transalpina* appeared, are elaborate and rather like church music in style, but such a one as his 'This sweet and merry month of May', which was said to be composed 'after the Italian vaine', is quite different. The little phrase of quavers which always goes with the words 'merry, merry' is as light-hearted as anything could be, and the broad passages to the words 'O beauteous Queen' bring the main idea of the poetry (the praise of Queen Elizabeth) into strong prominence.

Poets loved to make the Queen the subject of their verse, and musicians vied with them in this, eventually producing in 1603 (dated 1601) the most famous collection of English madrigals existing to this day, which was called *The Triumphs of Oriana*. It consists of madrigals by many of the most eminent men of the time, and the series was edited by one of the greatest of them, Thomas Morley. Whatever the subjects of the poems might be, whether they had to do with the loves of shepherds and shepherdesses or with nature and spring-time (the most favourite subjects), all had one feature in common: each one ended with a refrain such as

> Then sang the Nymphs and Shepherds of Diana.
> Long live fair Oriana.

A glance at a few numbers will both tell us who were the principal composers and give some idea of their work. The series opens with a fine madrigal by Michael East beginning 'Hence stars too dim of light' in which the poet fancies that the stars must pale before the beauty of his Queen, and the dignity of the whole music, especially the majesty of the two broad chords with which it opens, contributes to the splendid notion. In many cases we can see a direct attempt to illustrate the idea of the words, as in John Mundy's 'Lightly she tripped o'er the dales' which begins by four voices singing the same tune after one another with very dainty effect, or in John Benet's 'All creatures now are merry minded'. The last is more modern in sound than many, for the voices seem less independent of one another, and their movement is more clearly controlled by the use of certain chords:

Ex. 15

Birds o-ver her do hov - - - - - er.

This passage from it, for instance, in which the voices twine round a single chord of A to express the idea of hovering is unusual, and more like the later style of Purcell and Handel, when the parts were all made to conform to a definite key of which one chord was the centre and chief.

Thomas Morley's 'Arise! awake!' gives a good example of the way in which composers were beginning to make their tunes more permanent. Most of the earlier madrigalists did not treat their first idea as of special importance, and after the first words had been sung they did not reproduce the same musical figures. But here Morley brings the figure marked '*a*' into

almost every line except the refrain, and its charming lilt per-
vades the whole and gives it a feeling of continuity:

Ex. 16

John Willbye's 'The Lady Orianna' and Thomas Weelkes's
'As Vesta was from Latmos hill descending' (the latter is one
of those most often sung at the present day) are two particularly
fine madrigals for six voices, and the works of their composers
are surprisingly varied. The frank simplicity of Weelkes's 'Lo
country sports' and the delicate charm of Wilbye's 'Adieu
sweet Amarillis' contrast wonderfully with these stately madrigals in the *Triumphs*. Probably Weelkes's 'Vesta' gets its
present popularity from the close way in which the words are
illustrated throughout. Vesta descends and the 'maiden queen'
ascends, and both are realistically pictured in the downward
and upward movement of the music. Moreover the line 'then
two by two, and three by three together' is sung by two voices
on the first phrase, three on the second, and all six on the word
'together', and this quaint way of depicting the words never
spoils the flow of the music. It is managed with perfect artistic
skill.

### ORLANDO GIBBONS

One composer who did not contribute to the *Triumphs of Oriana*
must be noticed specially. ORLANDO GIBBONS (1583–1625),

whose brother Ellis Gibbons wrote two fine madrigals for the *Triumphs*, belonged to a musical family, and, like Tye, was educated as a chorister at King's College, Cambridge. He became organist of the Chapel Royal, and finally, only two years before his death, he was appointed organist of Westminster Abbey. These two appointments may be taken as a sign of the increasing importance of instrumental music in churches, for in the case of the Chapel Royal the position itself was a comparatively new one. There had been no organist in Tye's day.

Of Gibbons's madrigals, 'The silver swan', 'O that the learned poets', and 'Ah! dere heart' are still very popular, and they and others have a thoughtful, plaintive character which is quite Gibbons's own. He alone of the composers of his time seems to have cared deeply what words he set. Nymphs and shepherds and light-hearted verses with 'fa la' refrains had no attractions for him. Almost all his words are serious and many are sad. He certainly had a wonderful way of expressing melancholy sentiment in the melodies he found and in the way in which he combined them. For example, nothing could convey more thoroughly the idea of a questioning unrest than the beginning of the madrigal, 'What is our life' (Ex. 17).

His serious nature is no doubt the reason why he alone of his generation was able to write new and really valuable church music, suitable to the needs of the English liturgy and filled with the dignified and lofty spirit of the older Latin music. His service in F and certain of the anthems are truly polyphonic, in that all the voices have melodious music to sing, and yet the parts do not overlap in such a way as to hide the meaning of the words. In this respect he seems to have brought back the experience of the madrigalists to the service of the church.

Another new thing in Gibbons's church music calls for attention. He sometimes wrote important parts for instruments, especially viols, with the chorus or, more remarkable still, an accompaniment to a solo voice. A case in point is the anthem

'This is the record of John' (John i. 19) in which the questions and answers are sung by an alto voice (now generally by a tenor) and the answers are reinforced by the full choir. It is true that the music for the viols is not very different from that for the

Ex. 17

voices; in the solo passages the instruments merely weave a quiet background to the carefully accentuated words, but still the contrasts between solo, chorus, and orchestra show that Gibbons's mind was moving in a direction similar to that of the Italian operatic composers.

### INSTRUMENTS AND THE VOICE

The fact is another sign of the increasing interest in instruments. Composers would often publish their madrigals with a note on the title-page to say that they were 'apt for voices or viols', which meant that they might be played as we would play a string quartet, as pieces of pure music without words, or with one voice singing the words and the other parts played on viols. They also composed 'Fantasias' or 'Fancies' originally written for the viols. Some of the best of these were the work of Gibbons himself. His fantasias include passages which would be most inapt for voices, but which are perfect on the instruments, so that it is clear that in a quieter and less enterprising way Gibbons and other Englishmen were going through some of the same experiences which Monteverdi and the Italians had had.

Again the habit came into fashion of writing partsongs so that it was possible to perform them either by several voices or by one voice accompanied on the lute. They were generally called 'ayres' to distinguish them from the more complex madrigals, and of course the single essential voice was given more important music than the others which might be left out in favour of a lute. Numbers of charming 'ayres' of this kind were written by John Dowland, Robert Jones, Thomas Campion, and Philip Rosseter. Look at this beautiful one by Campion:

Ex. 18

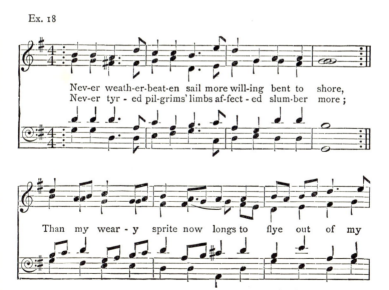

The tune of the treble voice is the all-important part of it; the chords underneath can be sung by three other voices or thrummed upon a lute with equal ease. The tune has the simplicity of the old folk-songs; it fits its words as beautifully as the early song by Adam de La Halle (see p. 8), but it is also clearly harmonized according to its key in a way which was quite beyond the powers of the medieval composers, and this power was the result of the polyphonic style being applied as a means of accompaniment.

The composers who wrote these songs, which very strikingly show, in comparison with the madrigals, the entirely different flavour of the Stuart school, were not always skilled musicians like Byrd and Morley and Gibbons. Dowland, indeed, was famous as a lute player, and had travelled to many of the courts of Europe, but others were rather poets who had enough musical knowledge and feeling to make tunes to go with their poetry. During the reign of the Stuarts and even under the Commonwealth the development of solo songs went on, and songs were joined with dances and instrumental music connected with plays and 'masques' (cf. p. 61). Lawes's music to

Milton's masque of *Comus* is the most well-known instance and one which you may still sometimes hear performed. The care which Lawes gave to the accurate accenting of words was rather like the Italian recitative of Monteverdi, but Lawes was in no other respect comparable to Monteverdi, for he had none of his commanding musical genius.

### KEYBOARD INSTRUMENTS

We have already seen music for sets of viols growing up into independent life and organs being used with the voices in churches. Needless to say, organists exercised themselves in composing for their instrument alone, and another sort of keyboard instrument had come into use in private houses and filled the place that the piano holds now. It was called the 'virginal' and is perhaps best described as a small kind of harpsichord (see p. 21). It is not always easy to tell whether the early English keyboard music was written for the organ or the virginal, and probably a great deal of it was played indifferently upon either, but nearly all the great composers of the time, Tallis, Byrd, Morley, Gibbons, and others wrote quantities of music for keyboard instruments. Much of it took the forms of dance-tunes such as 'Pavans' and 'Galliards', and these would naturally be for the virginal rather than the organ.

Fantasias and preludes, pieces which were a mixture of the style of choral music with scales and turns such as were found to lie well under the fingers, were also popular. But perhaps the most important kind of piece was the 'Air with Variations'.

Sometimes a folk-song, sometimes a church tune was taken as the air, and the composer would then add ingenious figures and new harmonies. The practice of writing variations led to the discovery of what we now call 'thematic development', that is to say, the power of carrying on and increasing the interest of a tune by placing its figures and rhythms in a number of new relationships.

The cleverest of the English writers for the organ and virginal was Dr. JOHN BULL. He was considered a very brilliant performer both at the court of Elizabeth I and on the Continent, and certainly his pieces show more of a genuinely instrumental style than most of the music of the time; scales, arpeggios, and broken chord passages, such as we often find in modern piano music, frequently appear in his variations, and sometimes he tried truly marvellous experiments in harmony, modulating through a number of keys. The most wonderful of these is a set of variations on an ascending scale of six notes (Ut, Re, Mi, Fa, Sol, La) in which the scale begins a tone higher each time, and so passes through modulations which seem strange even to modern ears.

If Bull was the cleverest, others wrote with more intimate feeling for what was really beautiful in music; Byrd's variations on 'Jhon come kisse me now' and Gibbons's on 'The woods so wilde' are lovely specimens of the style. We have seen the folk-song taken as the basis for church music and used in a quite unsuitable way (see pp. 10–11 and 31); in these and other pieces collected together in the Fitzwilliam Virginal Book the songs are set forth and expanded in a way which is natural and beautiful, since instead of hiding their origin the variations emphasize and enlarge it.

A truly original and thriving school of music for keyboard instruments was thus founded in Elizabeth's reign and carried on after it. Probably the Civil Wars and the Puritan rule did actually check its further growth, but it is unsafe to give political reasons for artistic changes. The art of the madrigalists was certainly exhausted, and the wave of musical enthusiasm in England was receding long before the trouble came. Once again England had to wait for a new impulse to come from abroad before her music could spring forth in fresh and still more varied forms.

## *Suggestions for Further Reading and Listening*

THE most important books suggested as supplementary reading at the end of Chapter I, which did not include English music, will have already served for the present chapter to a considerable extent. It may be just recalled here that they are vols. ii–iv of *The New Oxford History of Music*, and two works by Gustave Reese, *Music in the Middle Ages* and *Music in the Renaissance*. Both deal with English music only incidentally, of course, though generously; for an exclusive study the early chapters of Ernest Walker's *A History of Music in England* should be consulted, preferably in the new edition revised by J. A. Westrup, who is more sympathetic than the author towards early music of any school.

There are many valuable studies on various subjects and on single composers. The article in Grove's *Dictionary of Music* on 'Sumer is icumen in' gives a good deal of additional information on that early 'round'. E. H. Fellowes on *The English Madrigal Composers* and Peter Warlock on *The English Ayre* are indispensable. On Dunstable see Manfred Bukofzer's Preface to his edition of that master's work in *Musica Britannica*, vol. viii, some of which may also be played, though not very effectively, on the piano. There is a book on Marbeck (*Merbecke's Book of Common Prayer Noted*) by J. Eric Hunt, and there are works on Byrd by Frank Howes and on Orlando Gibbons by Fellowes.

For gramophone records readers should turn back to vols. ii–iv of *The History of Music in Sound* and select the English items which were not relevant to chapter i. There are many separate recordings of English madrigals from which a generous selection can be made; church music by Fayrfax, Byrd, Tallis, and others (there is a good selection issued under the aegis of the British Council) can also be well exhibited; and songs to the lute by Dowland are to be had, to which it is quite likely that those by other masters of that school have been or will be added.

# CHAPTER III

# ℳusic in ℱour ℭountries at the ℰnd of the Seventeenth ℭentury

## I. ITALY

W E saw that Monteverdi's operas were only one sign, though the most striking one, of the revolution which spread over the whole of the art of music in the seventeenth century. Before that time all music for voices was written in practically one style, that of the Church, since the secular madrigals were only a variation of the same type. Monteverdi's *Orfeo* suggests at least three ways of writing for the solo voice, recitative, expressive aria or melody, and coloratura (see p. 25), and also shows some of the wonderful things which instruments can do, both as a contrast to the voice and by themselves, as a means of illustrating the dramatic situation (e.g. the descent of Orpheus to the nether world).

### ORATORIO

In Italy the development of these different styles went forward very rapidly. GIACOMO CARISSIMI, who was born near Rome in 1605, did notable work in writing a number of oratorios on Old Testament subjects, such as *Jephte*, *Judicium Salomonis*, and *Baltazar*, which consist of recitatives, arias for solo voices, and choruses with, however, a much more slender instrumental accompaniment than the early composers of opera used. As they are not dramatic works the story which on the stage would be acted has to be told by the singers, and this is the most important difference existing between opera, or music with acting, and oratorio in which there is no acting. Let us take a modern example to make the difference quite clear. When Wagner in the last scene of *Götterdämmerung* wished to depict

Brünnhilde and her horse leaping into the flames which surround the funeral pyre of Siegfried he was able to do it by means of a very few bars of descriptive orchestral music, because the audience could see the whole thing acted on the stage, before their eyes, and all that the music had to do was to impress the meaning of it upon them by recalling the ride of the Valkyries and the fire music. But when Mendelssohn wanted to tell in oratorio how Elijah was taken up by a whirlwind into Heaven he had to write a great chorus on the words, 'And when the Lord would take him away to Heaven, Lo, there came a fiery chariot with fiery horses and he went by a whirlwind to Heaven'. The singers have to tell what is going on, and the rushing, excited character of the music has to picture the whole scene to the mind since it is not visible to the eyes.

Carissimi generally met the difficulty by making a tenor voice labelled 'Historicus' tell the story in recitative. At some of the more exciting parts of the story, however, he did just what Mendelssohn did in his *Elijah* and made the chorus take up the part of the historian. The principal characters are represented by solo singers as in opera, and in the dialogues between the characters Carissimi used the recitative very beautifully. He made his voices move by smoother intervals and arranged his harmonies much better than Monteverdi usually did, so that though his effects were less striking they were more genuinely beautiful. There is a splendid instance where Jephthah has told his daughter that she must die, and she has asked leave to go to the mountains and mourn with her companions. The daughter sings (Ex. 19). See how clearly the cadences at the end of each

Ex. 19

Plor - a - te, plor - a - te col - les, do - le - te, do -

le - te mon - - tes;    et in af - flic - ti -

- o - ne cor - dis me - i   u - lu - la - - - te.

Et in af - flic - ti - o - ne cor - dis me - i   u - lu -

CHORUS.

la - - te.   u - lu - la - te.

u - lu - la - - - te.

'Weep O hills, mourn O mountains!
And in the affliction of my heart lament!'

phrase mark the key. The first in A minor, the second in D, the third in E, and the fourth coming back to A with a lovely echo refrain to round it off. Then notice how genuinely pathetic the voice part is. The use of B flat in the cadence and the little turn on the second syllable of 'ululate' (lament) is perfectly expressed, and the whole, besides being true to the spirit of the words, is a beautiful bit of melody.

OPERA

Carissimi's works are more important for what they taught his pupils than for their own sakes, and of his followers the one who had greatest effect upon music as a whole was ALESSANDRO SCARLATTI (born 1659), who is said to have studied with him. This is just possible, but Carissimi died when Scarlatti was fifteen.

By the time that Scarlatti got to work the new kinds of music were being heard in all the big towns of Italy, but especially at the courts of princes and cardinals. Although the latter were churchmen by profession they often supported opera and other forms of secular music more ardently than the strictly church kinds of art, and the houses of some of the wealthy cardinals, usually members of the nobility who did not always serve the church for strictly religious reasons, were the resort of musicians anxious to secure the patronage of these great men for the performance of their works. It must be remembered that as soon as music left the church and ventured into the world at large, it had to depend for success upon its popularity, so that the style of music has been influenced at every time and at every place since the middle of the seventeenth century by the taste of the people for whom it was written, and consequently we must take this fact into consideration and try to find out the degree of importance which music had in the lives of these people. Opera had a particularly good chance of success in Italy at this time because not only were there princes, like Ferdinand III of Florence, who maintained private opera houses at their palaces, but public ones began to be opened in the principal towns, beginning with Venice (1637), which any one who could afford to pay for a seat might attend, and at which composers could get their works performed. The first public opera house in Rome was opened in 1671, and though the popes who were the reigning sovereigns of Rome did not always approve (and with some reason) of the conduct of the opera house, and this one was suppressed for a time by Innocent XI, such mishaps were merely a temporary check. So we find Scarlatti trying his fortune in various places, at one time sending an opera to Ferdinand de' Medici with a long letter to assure him that the music was 'pleasant and tuneful rather than learned', at another living at Rome under the patronage of Cardinal Ottoboni, or again setting off to Venice to direct the performance of a new opera there, or producing operas in Naples where he spent a great part of his life. The chances for composers were indeed many, but still they had to learn what sort of music would please their patrons, as Scarlatti's letter to Ferdinand shows. A great dramatic scheme, carried on with a huge, unwieldy orchestra, such as Monteverdi had used in *Orfeo*, was not likely to be very acceptable. Grand people who patronize opera, as well as people who pay for it, like to be entertained with 'pleasant and tuneful' music and gay and brilliant scenes on the stage, and often care much more to compare the performances of singers and to applaud their efforts than to follow the story of the drama or to consider whether the music is really appropriate. This was what Scarlatti found out, and that no doubt is the reason why, although he could write brilliant musical dialogues and did so in comic operas, his serious operas are mainly a series of songs joined together by recitative.

This defect, however, had its compensation, for Scarlatti learnt to write songs of a certain pattern more perfectly than any one had done before him. In doing so he had to establish certain laws of contrast, which now that they have been used over and over again seem so simple to us that it is hard to think that they were not always understood. It seems natural enough to us if a song in C major has first a tune in that key, then one modulating, as we say, to the key of G, and then repeats the first one in C. It is the simplest kind of ternary (threefold) form, and 'The Bluebells of Scotland' is a well-known instance of it. You can find plenty of others among hymn-tunes and old songs. Even the early song *L'homme armé* (see pp. 10–11) comes very near to being in a simple ternary form. Scarlatti did not invent the idea, but by writing hundreds of songs in operas and cantatas on this plan he taught himself and his successors several important facts: (1) that a great deal of variety and charm can be given by changing the key at the moment when a new melody is begun; (2) that the repetition of the first melody after the variety has been given helps to avoid any feeling of vagueness which the change of key alone would produce; (3) that in order to contrast one key with another it is necessary to make each key quite clear in itself, and the chords which do this most of all are the tonic and dominant. The type of song cultivated by Scarlatti and his successors, including Handel, is known as the '*da capo* aria', from the direction *da capo* ('from the beginning') shown at the end of the middle section to indicate that the first part is to be repeated.

Probably Scarlatti's songs did more than any music of their time to spread the new plan of writing in accordance with a key system which, as we saw, was quite foreign to the ideas of the old church composers. Scarlatti has been blamed for using the same pattern so constantly, and the fact that he did so would make any of his operas tedious to listen to nowadays if the music as such were less magnificent and the songs, though they belong to the same pattern, did not have tunes of very different characters. There are smooth and pathetic ones, bold and martial ones, lively and florid ones. The canzonetta 'O cessate di piagarmi' is quite a perfect little example of the form. The words ('O cease to wound me, O leave me to die') are very mournful, and the tune with its constantly repeated note, its lovely, drooping cadence, and the contrast between the principal minor key and the major one in the middle expresses their feeling beautifully. Another, 'Rugiadose, odorose, graziose violette' ('Dewy, scented, graceful violets'), is as light and dainty as a song can possibly be. You must hear them sung and played in order to realize how perfectly they are written, simple as they are, and to note how clearly the key of each phrase is marked by tonic and dominant cadences.

Since Scarlatti had practically given up all attempts to illustrate the dramatic ideas of his operas by the instruments of his orchestra, he used fewer instruments than Monteverdi. Their chief duty was to accompany the voice, but nevertheless he sometimes found out new and beautiful ways of combining them. He discarded the clumsy lutes and organs and used the harpsichord chiefly to accompany the recitative, so that the stringed instruments of the violin family became the basis of the orchestra, and they have kept their position to the present day. Sometimes he added effective parts for flutes, oboes, horns, and trumpets in the arias or in the overtures and other pieces for the instruments alone which occur in the course of an opera.

## INSTRUMENTAL MUSIC

Scarlatti must have found out a good deal about the use of stringed instruments from ARCANGELO CORELLI, whom he met at the house of Cardinal Ottoboni. Public concerts such as we have now were unknown in Italy at that time, but musicians, poets, and other artists often met together to perform and to listen to each other, and perhaps the most celebrated society of the kind was that called 'Accademia Poetico-Musicale' (the Poetic and Musical Academy) which met in the palace of this cardinal at Rome.

Corelli (1653–1713), the first great violinist of history, was a few years older than his friend Scarlatti. He devoted his whole life to playing his instrument and composing music for it and other stringed instruments, so that he gained a special knowledge of this kind of art from which men like Scarlatti, who were busy composing in every known form, must have learnt a great deal. Corelli's works are of two kinds. There are **sonatas** for one or two violins with a bass part to be played both by a violoncello and a harpsichord (the harpsichord player adding chords to fit with the other parts according to his discretion), and **concertos**, in which three solo players (two violins and a violoncello) play together accompanied by a band of violins, violas, violoncellos, and double basses, always supported by a harpsichord. Some of the sonatas, his earlier works, used to be played at the meetings of the 'Academia', of which both Scarlatti and Corelli became members in 1706. In the same year a young German, George Frederick Handel, visited Rome and attended some of the meetings. Since he listened to Corelli's work and learnt much from it, it will certainly be worth while for us to do so.

The sonatas generally contain four movements, a quick one and a slow one alternately, and each movement is divided into two sections. The first section gives out a melody which modulates into some other key at the cadence, and the second, beginning in that key, returns to the one from which the first started, using some fragments of the melody given out by the first and adding others. The form is called **binary** (twofold), and the difference between it and the **ternary** one of Scarlatti's songs is very important. The well-known hymn-tune by Thomas Tallis called 'Tallis's Ordinal' (Hymns A. & M., 78, &c.) is as simple an instance of the form as could possibly be found, for it consists merely of two musical sentences, the first of which modulates into the dominant key, while the second returns to the first or tonic key. It is interesting to remember that 'Tallis's Ordinal' was written about a hundred years before Corelli used the same principle for his sonatas. It allows space for a great deal of contrast, and yet the shape of the piece is perfectly clear without requiring any actual repetition. It was usual to play each section through twice, but that was only a matter of custom. Although the bare outline is the same in each case, there is plenty of change in the character of the pieces. This will be seen if we look particularly at one sonata—Op. 5 No. 8, in E minor (Chrysander's edition). This is one of the best-known of the solo sonatas. It begins with a prelude, a beautiful, slow melody in 3/4 time. Then follows a very lively one called

'Allemanda' (i.e. in the German style), of which we must quote the first phrase:

Ex. 20

You see at once that it is violin music. No voice could jump about in so sprightly a way, and it would be hard even to play such a tune on the piano because the hand would have to move such a long distance. But it is perfectly written for the violin, since a little movement of the bow reaches from the E string to the G string and back again quite easily. It shows how well Corelli understood the character of his instrument. Next there is a smooth and expressive tune called a 'Sarabanda' (a kind of Spanish dance), and finally there is a lively one called 'Giga' (we should call it a jig), in which again there are many passages which leap over long intervals and could only be made really effective on the violin. The movements are very short, for one of the things which composers had not yet learnt to do was to carry on the tunes and sustain the interest through long movements, but you will find that each of the four belongs clearly to the binary pattern, and each one has a strong, rhythmic character.

There is rather more variety of form in the concertos, for where many instruments played together it was possible to get more contrast between the solos and the full band, so that the same phrases of melody could be repeated by different instruments, much as they used to be in the old choral music of the madrigals. On the other hand Corelli's writing is less distinctly instrumental in the concertos, and sometimes one finds passages which remind one very strongly of choral music. An example is the opening of the eighth concerto, which looks and even sounds quite like a piece of contrapuntal church music of the old style. Such passages, however, are the exception in Corelli, and his music marks a turning-point in the life of instrumental music, for he gave it a stronger character than it had possessed before. Corelli did further service to his art by founding a great school of violinists who, as we shall see, carried on his principles in playing and composing for their instrument through the next century. Meanwhile his music was a model for his contemporaries, and it remains a delight for us today because of its lovely melody and its purity of design.

Alessandro Scarlatti certainly benefited by Corelli's work to this extent, that after he had heard his sonatas he wrote passages in his own works which were more exactly suited to the instruments than was his earlier music. Even the form of the overtures to his operas was to some extent affected by Corelli. Scarlatti generally wrote his overtures in three movements, an allegro, a slow movement, and a rhythmic dance to finish with. It is in the last movements that he seems to have been so delighted by the 'giga' of Corelli that he was forced to try to copy it. Scarlatti himself wrote some concertos for strings with a few wind instruments, as well as some sonatas, but in pure instrumental music his most important work was for the harpsichord. His pieces called 'toccatas' for this instrument are very fluent and brilliant, full of rapid passages which do not halt just at the moment when they are becoming interesting, as is so often the case in the older harpsichord music. Some of the toccatas are followed by fugues, and occasionally a dainty minuet, *corrente*, or other dance tune is added to complete the scheme.

No doubt these works, which are carefully fingered by Scarlatti, were written partly for the education of his son, Domenico, who became a great player and composer for that instrument. DOMENICO SCARLATTI was born in 1685, a year to be remembered by all musicians, since in it were also born G. F. Handel and J. S. Bach. He devoted himself to the harpsichord and wrote over five hundred extremely characteristic sprightly and beautiful pieces which he called *Essercizi* (exercises), which is precisely what they are, although at the same time they are in an early form of sonata, and they are now always so described. But the term 'sonata' which Corelli used, is only an instance of the rather puzzling fact that different things in music are often called by the same name. Domenico's 'sonatas' are generally in one movement, and the form is only like Corelli's in that it is binary. They are not made out of dance tunes, 'sarabandes' or 'gigues', but are rather more like toccatas (that is to say pieces written for the display of the player's skill), only they are written in the regular order of key which belongs to binary form. They are almost all quick movements, requiring the utmost skill and neatness of execution, and full of a brilliant gaiety and high spirits which was quite new to the music of the time. People who were used to the solemn beauty of church music or to the pomp of operatic overtures or arias must have been taken by surprise when young Scarlatti poured out these pieces full of glitter and humour, or possibly they did not think very much of them.

Nowadays we can see that these sonatas were far in advance of anything which had been written for the harpsichord, and their only fault is that they are so much in the same vein of feeling. Each one is quite perfectly worked out. Domenico modulates from one key to another with even more ease than his father had been able to do, and indeed often with an audacity that seems quite 'modern' even today. The musical ideas are more consistently carried out, and the ideas themselves are always fresh and frank. So, although they are ideally written for the harpsichord, pianists delight to play his sonatas on the piano at the present day, just as violinists delight in those of Corelli. A certain thoroughness seems to belong to both Scarlattis, father and son. They worked in narrow limits, but within those limits their work was wellnigh perfect.

## II. FRANCE

We saw in the first chapter that the French people were early in the field as makers of songs, and that they had special aptitude for setting music to poetry, so that the rhythm of the music should agree well with the metre of the verse. Towards the end of the seventeenth century the music of France became of importance to all the world, for the French people have the power of incorporating with their own what is pleasing to them of the art of other nations, and yet not losing their special characteristics. So when an Italian composer, Francesco Cavalli, who had been a pupil of Monteverdi, came to Paris in 1656 and performed operas of his own composition the French were pleased, but on the whole they thought that their own composers might do better than the Italians, and certain of them set to work to try.

Plays with music were no new thing to the Parisians, for, as we have seen, songs, dances, and acting had been companions ever since the days of Adam de La Halle, and at the court of Louis XIII *mascarades*, in which the actors danced and sang, were so fashionable that members of the court and even the King himself took part in them. But the idea of a whole play set to music in which all the words were sung instead of spoken was unfamiliar to the French people, and when they heard Cavalli's work they were not at all sure that they thought it an improvement on their own simpler songs and rhythmical dance-tunes.

### OPERA

However, the movement in favour of regular opera was too strong to be resisted, and even before Cavalli's appearance in Paris the Abbé Perrin, who had heard some of the works of the early Florentines, wrote a pastoral play, which Robert Cambert set entirely to music, and which was therefore the first French opera. It is known as *La Pastorale d'Issy*, from the country house at Issy near Paris where it was first performed in 1659, but as it is lost we do not know whether it originally had another title, as seems probable. What the Parisians seemed to have disliked about the Italian opera was the recitative, which with its lack of definite rhythm seemed to them like a sort of church plain-chant. Cambert adopted the style of the Italians to some extent, but in the works by him which have survived the recitative is certainly more melodious than theirs. Perhaps the actual style of the music mattered less to the grand people of the court than the subjects of the drama and the way in which they were presented. Here Perrin was very successful, for his plays were a mixture of classical fables, in which gods and goddesses, nymphs and fauns, shepherds and shepherdesses sported and made love in groves and silvan scenes. He made use of the same kind of imagery that one finds in the words of English Elizabethan madrigals, but he used it much more elaborately, and this was just the kind of thing which appealed to his audience. For if there was one thing more than another which was characteristic of the court life under Louis XIV, *le grand monarque*, as he was called, it was the pompous ceremony that was carried on. The very furniture which is nowadays called by the name of 'Louis Quatorze', the chairs and tables and escritoires with their bulging lines and heavy ormolu ornaments, show the grandeur amongst which people lived. But when people live constantly in an artificial atmosphere they sometimes like to play at leading a simple life, just as people who live very quietly like to read stories of princes and millionaires, or criminals and detectives, and to go to see royal processions. And so the court of Louis XIV would pretend to admire the beauties of quiet country life, and Watteau painted his celebrated pictures of grand ladies and gentlemen sitting on the grass under the trees, and Perrin's and Cambert's later operas, *Pomone* and *Les Peines et les Plaisirs d'Amour*, included scenes which were supposed to represent primitive life, but were really highly artificial, with troupes of dancers and brilliant scenery. There seemed to be every prospect that a poet and a composer who could hit the court taste so well, and who at the same time had genuine artistic powers, would make a permanent reputation, especially since in 1669 they had been granted the sole right of producing operas in French. But another man was destined to supersede them.

GIOVANNI BATTISTA LULLI (born 1632) was, as his name shows, an Italian by birth, but he became a Frenchman in the course of his remarkable career. Not only did he spend all his working life at the French court, where he managed to secure the monopoly which had been granted to Cambert, but he wrote work after work for the French stage completely in the French style. It is not surprising, therefore, that his name is better known in its French form as Jean-Baptiste Lully. To him belongs the credit of firmly establishing the kind of work which Cambert had begun, but unfortunately at the same time he must bear the discredit of having treated Cambert and other French artists exceedingly badly. Perhaps the fact that he was himself treated rather badly in early life may be some excuse for him, for he was brought to the household of a great lady, Mme de Montpensier, on account of his musical talents, and once placed there, his music seems to have been forgotten, and he was put to wash plates and do the duties of a scullion. Then he seems to have been turned out of the house because he had the impudence to make up sarcastic verses about his mistress. So it is not surprising that when he was about fifteen years old and had the luck to get a place in the King's band, he determined to work his own way up, and used even unscrupulous means of doing the best for himself. He had had no education in fair and honourable dealing. He was conscious of his lack of musical education, and did everything in his power to make this good by getting harpsichord lessons, and composing songs, dances, violin solos, and church music assiduously. However, he never felt his lack of moral training, but went on acting meanly to-wards other people whenever he could gain an advantage for himself. He remains one of the few men in the whole of musical history who wrote good music and were themselves despicable. In 1661-2 he received various appointments as musician to the King, and in 1664 he married the daughter of a court musical official, which seems to have been a profitable alliance for him.

The first event of artistic importance in Lully's life was his acquaintance with the great dramatist Molière, which began soon after his marriage. Lully provided incidental music for several of Molière's most brilliant comedies, such as 'Le Mariage forcé' and 'Le Bourgeois Gentilhomme', and thereby proved his skill as a composer of stage music. He also wrote a number of 'ballets', that is, sets of dances of various kinds for performance in the theatre, and gradually increased his popularity with the King and court, so that eventually he persuaded the King to transfer the patent in opera from Cambert to himself. From 1672 to 1687, when he died, he composed opera after opera, which were admired partly for their very genuine merits, and partly because by getting the right of producing operas entirely into his own hands he ousted all rivals. Poor Cambert had to leave the country, and he came to England and died here; but he was not the only one who was damaged by Lully's intrigues, for even Molière suffered by not being able to command sufficient music for his comedies. One would have expected that a man of Lully's stamp, having gained the public ear and successfully disposed of other competitors, would have merely produced what in the slang phrase are called 'pot-boilers', worthless works which thoughtless people enjoy for the moment; but though all his operas have too much of the court artificiality to be tolerated now, they were really important productions in their time. With the aid of Quinault, an admirable poet, Lully found subjects for his works of much more real dramatic power than those of Perrin and Cambert. Some were stories from Greek dramas very much modernized, such as Alcestis or Theseus; others were medieval romances such as Roland and Armida. Whatever their source, the stories were set much in the same way, and Lully was particularly successful in combining a really dramatic treatment of the story with the necessary dances, songs, and spectacular effects which were dear to the audience.

Like Alessandro Scarlatti he adopted certain fixed forms for various parts of his works, but they were different from those of Scarlatti. For instance, instead of the Italian overture in three movements like an instrumental concerto (see p. 59), Lully adopted a very concise form; a slow introduction led straight into a quick movement in which the various parts imitated one another in the manner of a fugue, ending up with a short coda in the slower time. This form, with or without the slow coda, became known as the French overture, and was very widely used by composers of many countries outside Italy, as we shall see later. It is very effective, for the solemn opening movement arouses the attention of audiences, and the quick movement,

Ex. 21

*Slow coda
follows.*

even when it is carelessly written, as Lully's sometimes were, is exciting and stimulating to the senses.

After the overture Lully always had an elaborate prologue, as Cambert had done, before the beginning of the opera proper, which was a kind of greeting ode to the King. In *Armide*, from which the overture is quoted above, and which we may take as

an example of Lully's style, two women singers, each attended
by a chorus, represented 'La Gloire' (glory) and 'La Sagesse'
(wisdom); they sang in praise of Louis, calling him 'the august
hero' and many other flattering names. This was followed by a
ballet of three dances—an 'entrée', 'menuet', and 'gavotte en
rondeau'. It was largely as a writer of dance tunes that Lully had
made his success early in life, and when one plays those which
appear in *Armide* and the other operas it is easy to see why
they were so popular. They have nothing like the fluent
grace of the Italian tunes such as Corelli wrote in his sonatas,
but they are very compact, neat, and simple: the sort of thing
one could hum as one went home, and yet rarely quite commonplace and never actually vulgar. The 'gavotte en rondeau'
is a very good specimen with its precise rhythm, its strong

Ex. 22

harmonies, and the clear feeling for balance of form which makes it always return to the first little tune after each of the contrasting ones.

The story of Armide and Renaud (or Armida and Rinaldo, as they were called by Tasso) has been as popular with opera composers as that of Orpheus and Eurydice, and as so many great men have used it, we will describe it in detail. The story dates from the time of the Crusades, and is the legend of a Syrian sorceress who was supposed to live in an enchanted palace and to lure knights to her, where they became so captivated by her charms that they forgot everything else. In the first act of Lully's opera the sorceress is seen in her palace; she receives a visit from Hidraot, the prince of Damascus, and together they plot to decoy Renaud, a very powerful knight. The entrance of Hidraot and his suite is accompanied by a spirited march rather like those of Handel (e.g. the march in *Scipione*), and there are of course dances performed by the suites of Armide and Hidraot. But all this is suddenly interrupted by a messenger who, in a truly dramatic recitative, tells how Renaud has rescued the prisoners of Armide, whereupon the sorceress and Hidraot vow vengeance on him, and the scene ends. In the next act Renaud, overcome by the spell, falls asleep by the water's edge; and here there is a descriptive piece of music for stringed instruments muted which is rather remarkable, for it suggests the effects of musical colour which have become so frequent in modern opera but which were rarely used in Lully's day. Then follows a pretty ballet of water-nymphs who sing and dance round Renaud, and finally Armide enters and sings a song of triumph at the capture. However, in Act III Armide discovers that she in turn is in love with Renaud, and she summons 'Hatred', who appears with all the passions of cruelty, vengeance, and rage; they dance and sing and call out 'non, non' (Ex. 23) on two detached chords with an effect which is rather like Elgar's demons in *The Dream of Gerontius*.

In Act IV two friends of Renaud's come armed with a magic

shield of diamonds and a golden sceptre to rescue him, but they
meet with various difficulties, and only in the fifth act succeed
in breaking the spell and tearing Renaud away. In this last act
in the enchanted palace the attendants of Armide are seen
dancing before Renaud to an elaborate Passacaglia, that is a

Ex. 23

Non!    non!

dance in which one phrase is repeated constantly in the bass,
while all sorts of variations of melody and rhythm are played
by other intruments over the various repetitions of the bass
(see Purcell, pp. 80–82).

Lully took for his bass the first four notes of the descending
scale of G minor, a very simple phrase which other composers
used in the same way, and wrote a remarkable number of variations which get more and more interesting as they proceed.
The scene is very effective, and he evidently intended it to be
something like what Wagner wrote much more graphically in
later years in the Venusberg music of *Tannhäuser*. When
Renaud is finally rescued, Armide sings a lament which opens
with a vigorous piece of recitative that actually sounds like
a cry of pain and horror:

Ex. 24

Re-naud!    Ciel!    O mor-tel-le pei-ne!

and so the opera ends.

Lully's airs are shorter and less developed into definite form
than those of Scarlatti and the other Italians, and they have
scarcely any variety of modulation or contrast of one key with
another; but they fitted better into the operatic scheme than

those of the Italians did, for the course of the story was never long interrupted by a single song. The beautifully smooth melody, 'Bois épais', from the opera *Amadis*, is an excellent example of Lully's vocal style.

Lully's selfish methods of dealing brought musical matters in France very much to a standstill when he died in 1687, for only one or two of his own pupils had had any practical experience in stage music at all, so that all his successors could do was to try rather feebly to copy his work. Not that it would be fair to blame Lully entirely for this. If any one of the court musicians had been a man of genius the death of Lully would have been his opportunity; but there was no genius ready to take up the work, and it was certainly Lully's doing that there were so few capable craftsmen. Jean-Philippe Rameau, the man who was destined eventually to carry on French opera and break through some of the formal traditions which hung round it as a court entertainment, was at this time only a baby of four years old. We shall see what he did later. Meantime there was only one branch of music which was cultivated with any important result, and that was music for the harpsichord or *clavecin*, as the French called it.

## MUSIC FOR THE HARPSICHORD

FRANÇOIS COUPERIN (born 1668) was a member of a family of French musicians, many of whom held good positions as organists, though they did not, like Lully, fight for high places. A few years after Lully's death François obtained the appointment of organist in the private chapel of the famous palace at Versailles. Of course he, like all other Parisians, was thoroughly acquainted with Lully's music, and in fact he arranged a number of Lully's most famous ballet dances for his favourite instrument, the harpsichord, to which he devoted himself as faithfully as did Domenico Scarlatti (see p. 60). Couperin's most valuable work includes sets of dances called *ordres*, in which a number of tunes in various styles are placed together so as to make very effective contrasts. *Ordres* are in fact suites.

Though these dances were founded on the style of Lully, yet they are much more delicate and intimately beautiful than his. This is natural, not only because Couperin was by far the greater genius, but also because Lully's were written to be danced to and Couperin's to be listened to. Moreover, instead of being written for an orchestra they were written for one instrument, and that the one which he loved and had studied very closely. Couperin knew that every little turn of phrase and rhythmic figure would be heard when played on his harpsichord, whereas Lully knew that only the general effect of his tune would be noticed when people in glittering dresses were dancing to it on the stage. Couperin was an imaginative man who was not merely content to make graceful tunes or even satisfied to make his music for the harpsichord perfect in design, as Domenico Scarlatti his contemporary in Italy was. He liked to connect his pieces with ideas that could describe their character. So besides calling them by the name of the dance to which they belonged, such as courante, sarabande, gavotte, menuet, or gigue, names which belonged alike to every composer, he often invented special descriptive titles. In his first *ordre* the sarabande is called *La Majestueuse*; it uses large and dignified chords and some very bold discords. That in the second, called *La Prude*, is much less enterprising, and a very beautiful one in the third *ordre* is called *La Lugubre*. At other times he would leave the recognized dance rhythms altogether and write pieces with all sorts of fancy titles, some of which seem really appropriate, such as the *Cuckoo*, whose double note can always be heard running through the pieces called by his name, or *Les Petits Moulins à vent* ('The Little Windmills'), whose perpetual movement is figured in a graceful little piece in flowing semiquavers. There is a remarkable set of little pieces called *Les Folies françoises, ou Les Dominos*, each of which represents some side of human nature, such as modesty, ardour, hopefulness, fidelity, perseverance, languor; and while some seem to have very little connexion with their subject, others, like *La Coquetterie*, in which the time changes no less than six times in sixteen bars, are full of delightful humour and insight. The idea underlying *Les Folies* is very like that of Schumann's *Carnaval*, in which each number pictures some particular character in a whimsical way.

Couperin, therefore, pointed out another direction to which music could turn, the illustration of ideas and subjects not connected with it by words sung or scenes acted, and this direction, which we now call 'programme music', is of immense importance to us at the present day.

## III. ENGLAND

When Charles II returned from his 'travels', as he called his exile during the Commonwealth, he brought a complete change of life and manners into London which had many undesirable features and some good ones. There can be no doubt that his coming was good for music, for the Puritan rule had forbidden theatres and suppressed cathedral services, so that the grand old church music of Byrd and Gibbons had been long silenced, and the new music of the theatre, which was developing in Italy and France, had made no strong mark here. Charles had spent some time at the French court, and though in 1660, when he returned to England, the opera of Lully had not begun, he had enjoyed the gay dances and ballets and *mascarades* of the French, and heard the early church music of Lully, which was scarcely less secular in rhythm and spirit than his theatre music. The services of the Chapel Royal were again reopened, and a choir was brought together under the mastership of Captain Cook, a musician who had got his military title by serving in the army of Charles I against the Parliamentary forces. It is not wonderful that the efforts of Cook and the other musicians who had survived the Commonwealth seemed old-fashioned and dull to the light-hearted king. Their music seems dull enough to serious musicians nowadays, for all they could do was to copy the form and manner of the older writers, and there was no real genius among them.

English music required a fresh stimulus from without, and

this was given to it in various ways by the restoration of Charles II. He tried to bring it about directly by sending one of the choristers of the Chapel Royal to France to study music under Lully. This was Pelham Humfrey, a very clever boy, who picked up the manner current in France, and returned to England 'an absolute *monsieur*', as Samuel Pepys tells us, and very proud of his achievement. But he only lived until the year 1674, seven years after his return, and though he wrote a good many anthems and songs, his music is chiefly important because it helped to show the new way to his successors. Captain Cook seems to have been very shrewd in finding boys of real musical talent for his choir, since apart from Humfrey a great many of his choristers distinguished themselves as composers.

The three most important of them were MICHAEL WISE (born 1648), JOHN BLOW (born 1649), and HENRY PURCELL (born 1659), who was the greatest musician of his time and with whom this chapter must be chiefly concerned. All these must have profited more or less by the experience of Humfrey in France, for Wise and Blow were his contemporaries in the choir, and when Cook died and Humfrey succeeded him for a few years, Purcell was a chorister under him. But Purcell was less indebted to Humfrey than were the two older men, for by the time that he was growing up French music and even Italian music was becoming fairly well known. Though King Charles was determined not 'to go on his travels again' he was determined also not to be cut off from continental life, and the coming of visitors from abroad and the constant intercourse with France did good service to art and music in particular, however injurious the connexion might be from a political point of view. Blow succeeded Humfrey as master of the children of the Chapel Royal in 1674 when Purcell was still one of the 'children'. He also therefore was Purcell's teacher, and when his distinguished pupil grew up he seems to have given up the post of organist of Westminster Abbey, which he held together with that of the Chapel Royal, to Purcell in the year 1680. However, Purcell died in 1695, and then Blow returned to the Abbey and held the position there as organist till his death in 1708. Wise held hardly less distinguished appointments as a member of the Chapel Royal choir both as a boy and as a man, organist for some time of Salisbury Cathedral and afterwards master of the choristers at St. Paul's Cathedral in London.

All the music which you are likely to hear either by Blow or Wise is contained in their church anthems. Blow's 'I was in the Spirit' and 'I beheld and lo a great multitude', and Wise's 'Prepare ye the way of the Lord' and 'The ways of Zion' are some which you may often hear in cathedrals. They are quite different from the old church music of Gibbons, for example, for he, even when he used instruments, made them behave like voices, but Blow and Wise often made their voices behave like instruments. They sing runs and rhythmical tunes and especially figures containing this curious jerky rhythm (A):

Ex. 25

Thou know'st my down - - - - sit - ting.

in Blow's 'O Lord, Thou hast searched me out', which is almost like a comical imitation of a heavy man sitting down suddenly. Altogether, the restraint and solemnity of church music seems to have given way to a kind of music which could express much more than the old, but often expressed ideas and feelings which do not specially belong to church music. Still there are fine and noble passages in their music, ranging from Blow's dignified 'God is my hope', a solid piece of work for a choir of eight parts or voices, to Wise's pathetically beautiful anthem, 'Thy beauty O Israel', the lament of David for Saul and Jonathan. Often one feels that their music does not continue long enough in one mood. Their anthems are broken up into a number of little movements of various kinds, and no sooner is one idea fairly started than the movement ends and another begins. This scrappiness seems characteristic of all the Restoration composers, Purcell as much as any of them, and no doubt it came from the fact that these composers were finding out how to express feelings and thoughts which were new to music in this country, and they had scarcely time to consider principles of artistic arrangement very closely.

Purcell does not seem to have had any special advantages in life which Blow and Wise did not share, except the advantage of being ten years younger and so profiting by their experience. He came of a musical family, however; both his father and his uncle were appointed as gentlemen of the Chapel Royal at the restoration of the King, and he had several brothers, the youngest of whom, Daniel, made quite a reputation as a composer. Henry Purcell, like Blow, lived all his short life as a London musician, with few events of importance to mark it except the productions of his very numerous compositions and the one fact of his appointment as organist of Westminster Abbey in 1680. His career extended over the reigns of Charles II, James II, and the joint reign of William and Mary, and the composition of Queen Mary's funeral music was one of his last duties. What gives him his acknowledged place as a great composer, and makes him often spoken of as the greatest of English composers, is the extraordinary readiness with which he seized on every known form of composition and wrote fine work in it. He did not specialize in any one branch, but wrote quantities of music for the church, for the theatre, for the concert-room (which now first became an established institution in London), and chamber music (that is, music for performance in private houses), songs, dialogues, and instrumental works; and whatever he touched had a certain strong, fresh individuality which marked his work as distinct from that of any other man. The influence of older and of contemporary composers is often clear, and the fact that he made use of so many influences is not the least part of his skill. The old English church composers make themselves felt in the best of his church music. Lully's methods appear in his theatrical overtures, dances, and songs, and he acknowledged that his sonatas for stringed instruments were built on Italian models, and yet he never seems to be copying or writing at second hand; he builds up his own style upon the work of his predecessors.

The Englishman whose work seems to have influenced him most directly was MATTHEW LOCKE (born about 1630), the composer who wrote the processional music with which Charles II was brought back to London at the Restoration. Locke was also the composer of suites for violins which Mr. Pepys tells us in his Diary that he loved to play. Still more important, Locke composed certain operas which were given in London theatres, and he stoutly maintained in a preface to one of them that if only English musicians were given the opportunity they could excel in the production of operas equally with their fellows in Italy and France. His pioneer work for English opera was an incentive to Purcell, who wrote an 'Elegy on the Death of his worthy friend Mr. Matthew Locke' (1677) which begins with the words 'What hope for us remains now he is gone?'.

### PURCELL'S CHURCH MUSIC

Purcell wrote a large number of anthems for singing in church. It is generally supposed that those for voices with organ accompaniment only were written for the daily services of Westminster Abbey. Such are 'Save me, O God', 'Thy word is a lantern', and the eight-part chorus 'Hear my prayer', very beautiful pieces of choral writing but comparatively short. His longer anthems, partly accompanied by strings and with overtures and interludes for strings, were written for the Chapel Royal at Whitehall, where the King's band of string players took part in the service. Some of these are very splendid works and too rarely heard in their completeness now because we do not often have an orchestra to play in church, and they are difficult to fit into a choral concert, although splendidly effective there. One of the greatest of them is the anthem for the coronation of James II, 'My heart is inditing'.

Perhaps his most celebrated piece of church music is the festival setting of the Te Deum and Jubilate in D for voices, strings, trumpets, and organ. This great work sums up all the new characteristics which belong to the church music of the Restoration composers, and is so important that every one who wishes to understand the differences between their music and that of the older school of Byrd and Gibbons must study it. What strikes one at once is the wonderful variety of expression it contains. A few examples from the first few pages will show this, and others can be added.

First look at the theme of the instrumental introduction which is that sung by the voices afterwards to the words 'We praise Thee'. It is a march-like phrase, played by trumpets and violins alternately, as unlike as possible to the serene calm of Gibbons's Te Deum in F, or Byrd's Short Service, but giving the feeling of a great and moving procession. Next notice the way in which the voices mount up the notes of the chord of D proclaiming the word 'All' and finally sing it together on a brilliant sounding chord accompanied by all the instruments. Then at 'the Father everlasting' the voices for the first time move in smooth and flowing counterpoint as though those words brought the composer back to the more solemn thought which continually held the minds of the older writers. The big exclamations of the word 'Holy' by the whole choir while two treble voices repeat 'continually do cry', and the broad choral phrase to give the idea of 'Majesty', are further examples of Purcell's remarkable variety. Almost every page shows his keen sympathy with the spirit of the words, and perhaps the most striking part of the work is the alto solo 'Vouchsafe, O Lord'. This (in D minor) is in a kind of very free recitative. Its phrases are full of tender feeling. Notice especially the long phrase on the first 'O Lord', and the descending fifths on the repetitions of the same words. Coming as it does between two massive choruses in the major key this solo is particularly appealing.

One cannot fail to notice, however, how very little actual contrast of one key with another there is in this and in a great deal of Purcell's music. Where such changes are used they are generally from the major into the minor mode and back again, and the relation between the tonic and the dominant major keys is never used with the ease and mastery which the Italians, Scarlatti for example, acquired. But though the modulations are rather vague the harmonies are very rich, and the only fault in the spontaneous flow of the melody is the frequent use of the jerky rhythm $\left(\text{♩. ♪ ♩. ♪}\right)$ which we remarked in Blow's anthem.

### ST. CECILIA AND OTHER ODES

This Te Deum was written for the Festival of St. Cecilia, who was and is still regarded as the patron saint of music, and an interesting set of circumstances led to its composition. There was an old custom in many countries of celebrating the saint's day (22 November) with music, and in 1683 a scheme was started in London for holding a festival service in a city church on that day, and giving a public performance of an ode in praise of St. Cecilia and the art of music in Stationers' Hall. It was for the service eleven years after the first celebration that the Te Deum and Jubilate were written, but meanwhile Purcell had been connected with the secular part of the festival, and in fact wrote the first ode in 1683.

These performances mark the beginning of what has been the most important form of music-making in England for not far from three hundred years, the choral concert. It is interesting to remember that as Italy led the way in opening public opera houses, England can take credit for the first establishment of public concerts. The earlier odes were written on rather a small scale. Purcell set some doggerel verses, 'Welcome to all the pleasures', by a man called Fishburn, using a four-part chorus, solo voices, and stringed instruments. The work began with an overture, written in the manner of Lully's operatic overtures, and short songs and choruses were contrasted with artistic effect. The first ode was a great success, and in the following year Blow wrote one on much the same lines. These odes are really the beginning of secular cantata form in England which composers such as Parry and Elgar have cultivated. They were

continued more or less intermittently until in 1692 Purcell
wrote one which is on a much grander scale than any of the
others. He had been gaining experience in this sort of work by
writing numerous odes on other occasions, such as the birth-
days of members of the royal family, and so being provided
with an efficient libretto, 'Hail, bright Cecilia', a poem by Dr.
Brady (who is celebrated for his part in 'Tate and Brady's
Psalms'), he produced a work which surpassed all previous
efforts. Besides the stringed instruments of the orchestra he
used flutes, oboes, trumpets, and drums, and instead of the
short Lullian overture he wrote a long one in several movements, more in the Italian sonata style. After the overture the
bass solo declaims the words 'Hail, bright Cecilia' in a dignified recitative, and the chorus takes up the theme and carries
it on in magnificent fashion. The strong, free writing for the
chorus, the powerful harmonies in the recitatives, the vigorous
airs for the solo voices, such as 'The fife and all the harmony
of war', make this work a triumph of art in a direction which
had not yet been attempted by the musicians of any country.

A comparison of 'Hail, bright Cecilia' with the Te Deum
shows that almost the only difference of style between them is
the fact that the individual movements of the ode are much
longer and more fully developed than are those of the Te Deum.
Let us see how he did this. The song 'The fife and all the harmony of war' will show us one of his means. The alto voice
starts with a martial tune six bars long to the accompaniment
of trumpets and drums, and after an instrumental interlude it
is repeated and then carried on with running passages in the
manner of the Italian 'coloratura' aria, till it reaches a cadence on
the dominant (A). The song is continued by similar passages
which keep up the general feeling of the original tune without
ever repeating it, and cadences are made which touch on other
keys without actually modulating into them or departing for
any long passage from the principal key of D. In songs of this
sort Purcell had no fixed plan to work upon as the Italians had
in their ternary form, and so he had to rely more upon his own

invention in each case. Sometimes he required a more definite plan, and then he often used the form known as the ground bass. The bass song 'Wondrous machine', a song in praise of the organ supposed to be St. Cecilia's own instrument, will show you what a 'ground bass' really is. The first two bars for bass instruments only make a sort of groundwork for the whole song. They are repeated over and over in the bass while the voice and the other instruments add melody and harmony above them. In the middle, however, the ground bass changes its key to that of G major, and then there is a repetition of the first part, so that this song is a combination of the ground bass with ternary form (see Lully, p. 70).

<h2 style="text-align:center">THEATRE MUSIC</h2>

Purcell got his first chance of writing for the theatre at about the time that he became organist of Westminster Abbey, but what he then wrote was not an opera, only incidental music to a play. Thenceforward he went on writing such music in large quantities, always hoping, like Matthew Locke before him, for the fuller opportunity which a well-equipped opera house with a company of singers and players to produce new operas would bring. That hope was never fulfilled, but none the less a play was hardly considered complete without the introduction of music and dances. When new plays were written authors would provide opportunities for music, and when old ones were revived, such as Shakespeare's *Midsummer Night's Dream*, they would be altered and even shamelessly rewritten to make room for the display of song and dance, generally called a 'masque' (cf. the *mascarades*, pp. 46 and 61). Purcell wrote a great quantity of this music, such as the incidental music with the charming masque in the last act of *Dioclesian* (1690), a version of a play by Beaumont and Fletcher, which was advertised as 'being in the manner of an opera', and also that to *The Fairy Queen* (1692), which was a version of *A Midsummer Night's Dream*. Most important among them was Dryden's play, *King Arthur*, which was written for musical treatment: Purcell's music to it is so elaborate and often so genuinely dramatic that it only requires continuity to be a complete opera. Overtures, dances, and songs flowed from his pen with amazing ease, and it is not surprising that he often repeated himself and often adopted a rather stereotyped form, but still the fertility of his invention is very remarkable, much more remarkable for instance than that of Lully, who was doing the same sort of work at the same time in Paris.

Purcell produced only one real opera, that is a work in which a whole play is set to music, and that was the beautiful *Dido and Aeneas*. Curiously enough this was written for performance in a school of young ladies kept by a man named Priest, a fashionable dancing-master, who also used to arrange the dances at theatres for which Purcell composed.

The story of the love of the hero Aeneas for Dido, Queen of Carthage, their separation by witchcraft, and her death, is told in wonderfully pure and moving music. The overture is so exactly in the form which Lully laid down that it should be compared closely with his overture to *Armide* (pp. 65–67). Notice the greater power of Purcell's harmonies in the slow movement. The little by-episodes, the choruses and dances of witches, who plot against the lovers, and the merry-making of the sailors, have any amount of point and character, and give the necessary stage contrast, besides fulfilling their original purpose of showing off the acquirements of Mr. Priest's pupils.

One song, 'Dido's Lament', is particularly worthy of study, since it is probably the most moving song that Purcell ever wrote, and it is unsurpassed by anything of the kind which had been written by composers of other countries at this date. Like so many of Purcell's best songs it is written upon a 'ground bass', in this case a wonderfully pathetic theme of descending semitones. Above the solemn repetitions of this the voice sings a broad melody. Notice especially the drooping fifths on the word 'trouble' wherever it occurs, and the words 'Remember me' sung pensively on a single note (D), which rises to the high G when the feeling becomes most intense just before the end.

The chromatic harmonies (the chord of the seventh, ninth, and inversions) are also very striking, for they show that Purcell realized what strength of expression such things give at a time when they were scarcely appreciated by musicians in general.

*Dido and Aeneas* is sufficient to show that he had a real genius for this sort of art, and if he had lived to write other complete operas the course of that form of music in England must have been a good deal more distinguished than has actually been the case. As it was *Dido and Aeneas* could make little more than a passing impression, and the patchwork system of plays with incidental music continued its vogue until quenched by the coming of Italian opera to London.

### INSTRUMENTAL MUSIC

One more branch of Purcell's art must be noticed before we take leave of him, and that is his music for instruments alone. In the eventful year (1683) in which the Cecilian celebrations were started, Purcell published twelve sonatas 'of three parts', that is, for two violins, violoncello (or viol da gamba) with harpsichord accompaniment, in which he said he had 'faithfully endeavoured a just imitation of the most famed Italian models'. It is not certain what Italian works Purcell had seen, certainly not Corelli's, whose first book of sonatas was published in the same year, but when we take this fact into account his achievement in this direction is certainly very great. Ten others were published by his widow two years after his death, which are finer and richer in detail than the earlier ones. In neither do we find the intimate knowledge of what suits the stringed instruments which was so conspicuous in Corelli's works, nor is there the same grace of melody and definiteness of design, but they are full of fine writing, bold, sometimes crude harmonies, clever and humorous imitations between the parts, and strong contrasts between slow and quick, grave and gay movements.

Purcell's harpsichord music, too, consisting of suites and lessons, sets of clear, simple little pieces often in dance forms, show that the English musician was as much alive to the possibilities of keyboard music as were his companions in Italy and France (see pp. 60 and 71–73). It must have seemed as though Purcell could do everything for his art, and as though his genius were inexhaustible and untiring when all hopes of further achievement were suddenly cut short. He died after a short illness on 21 November 1695, the eve of St. Cecilia's Day, whose festival he had celebrated so often and so well, and he was buried in Westminster Abbey, where you may see his grave in the south choir aisle close to the organ.

## IV. GERMANY

So far the states of Central Europe collectively called Germany have had little of importance to add to the story of the growth of music, not because there was ever a time when the German races were unmusical, but because a number of causes kept them from taking the lead in the earlier artistic developments in which Italy, France, and England were all prominent in varying degrees. The geographical and political conditions combined to keep Germany back. It was a vast tract of country cut into innumerable states very much isolated from one another, and without acknowledged centres of culture such as Italy possessed in Rome, Florence, and Venice, or France in Paris. So although a great deal of music was composed by Germans, from the time of the Meistersinger and Minnesinger onward, the rest of the world heard very little of their efforts. Then, again, the religious disturbances in Germany checked the growth of church music at a time when that kind of work was at its best elsewhere. Luther published his famous protest against the teachings of Rome in 1517, that is some years before Palestrina was born, and those parts of Germany where Protestant doctrines prevailed had therefore no use for his complex and mystical style of choral music.

### CHURCH MUSIC

They had to learn to write church music of quite another kind, to compose or adapt tunes such as ordinary people who were not skilled musicians could sing to the accompaniment of the organ. The Reformation in Germany was much more drastic than in England, for though English Protestants persecuted Catholics and Catholics burnt Protestants when they got the chance, in the end this country settled down to a compromise which laid down no hard and fast rules as to how the artistic side of worship should be conducted. But in the Lutheran churches the principle that the music like the words must be such as the people could understand and join in was so far insisted upon that almost all existing music except some of the old plainsong hymn-tunes became inadmissible. We must go back, therefore, and trace the advance of music in Germany from an earlier date than the latter part of the seventeenth century, which we have been studying in other countries. Composers, headed by Luther himself and his friend Johann Walther, began to write simple hymn-tunes called by the Germans *Choräle*, and to adapt old church tunes and folk-songs for the purpose. Some are well known in English churches, such as the one called Luther's hymn and translated as 'Great God, what do I see and hear' (A. & M. 52), which comes from a hymn-book of 1537, or the lovely tune sung to 'O sacred Head, surrounded' (A. & M. 111), the work of Leo Hassler, or the almost equally beautiful tune 'Innsbruck' (A. & M. 86), adapted from an old folk-song. These tunes and many like them became very dear to German Protestants, and their musicians would play them on the harpsichord and write variations upon them or add ornamental passages and counterpoints to the simple tunes, so that from them sprang both the vocal church music and the instrumental music of Germany as it appeared at the end of the seventeenth century in the works of J. S. Bach.

Hassler himself was a musician of the older school, and most of his work, such as the Mass for eight voices, was written in the polyphonic style like that of Palestrina, but the beautiful chorale mentioned above, though intended to be a secular song, became one of the very foundations of Protestant church music, when later it was set to a favourite Passion hymn.

A still more striking figure in early German music is that of Heinrich Schütz, who was born in Saxony in 1585, and lived to a great age. He was one of the first musicians who realized that it ought to be possible, in some way or other, to combine all the best characteristics of the various kinds of music which, as we have seen, were leaping into existence at the beginning of the seventeenth century. No doubt the fact that his father was a man of some social position, and that Heinrich was given the benefit of a university education, as well as the advantage of study in Italy under Giovanni Gabrieli at Venice and a certain amount of foreign travel, enabled him to take a broader view of music as a whole than the ordinary German musician was able to take. Schütz was able to study and admire both the choral music of Palestrina and the new dramatic ideals of Peri, Monteverdi, and others. He saw that it should be possible to use the vivid expression of the new style without sacrificing all the grandeur and dignity of the old. In 1614 he obtained the appointment of *Kapellmeister* (i.e. chief court musician) to the Elector of Saxony, whose court resided at Dresden; he was particularly required to reorganize the music both sacred and secular upon Italian models. This practically meant that he had to know the best music of every kind that had been written; it did not mean that in his own compositions he had to copy any one style slavishly. He wrote a great quantity of sacred motets for voices and instruments combined, and an oratorio on the subject of the Resurrection appeared not many years after his appointment, in which it is curious to see choruses of a severe and church-like type joined with realistic, descriptive passages for the instruments. The story is told in free recitative by a single voice just as in Carissimi's oratorios (see p. 51). Schütz also made experiments in purely secular opera with *Dafne*, set to a German version of the libretto of Peri's work, produced at a court performance at Torgau, and also wrote an Orpheus ballet on much the same principle. (Both these works are lost.) But most important were four settings of the story of the Passion according to the four Evangelists, which he wrote late in life.

The Catholic custom of singing the Passion story in Holy Week was one of the parts of the service that England lost at the Reformation and Germany kept, with merely the difference that the words were sung in German instead of in Latin as formerly. But whereas in the Latin Passions the story and words of the chief characters were intoned to the traditional plainsong, and only the words of the crowd were set to short dramatic choruses, in the German Passions of Schütz the words of the story and the conversations are set to free recitatives which are so well joined with the choruses that the whole becomes a complete work of art instead of a patchwork between traditional and original music. This is a very important difference, for it brought about an entirely new and very beautiful kind of church music which reached its highest point later on in the works of J. S. Bach (see pp. 112 et seq.).

The long series of wars, generally known as the Thirty Years War, between the Emperor and the Catholic cause on the one hand and the various Protestant interests on the other, are often put forward as one reason why German music developed slowly, but since Heinrich Schütz carried on his work in the midst of them, it would seem that battles and bloodshed are not a very effective bar to artistic work when a man of real genius is concerned. It was, however, more in the latter part of the century, when the country was settling down, that music became a definite part of the life of every German town of consequence, and the organists in the churches and the town musicians became important as composers and performers.

Many members of the family of Bach were notable town musicians in the small towns of Thuringia—Erfurt, Arnstadt, and Eisenach—and from them eventually sprang one of the greatest musicians of all time, JOHANN SEBASTIAN BACH. The names and doings of the various members of the Bach family have all been carefully recorded for the sake of the great man who belonged to it, but in many other parts of Germany, particularly in the north, there were families and individuals whose names are forgotten, but who did the same permanent and sterling work in cultivating the musical taste of their countrymen by their excellent playing on the viols and the organ. Reinken, the organist of St. Catherine's at Hamburg (1654), is remembered because J. S. Bach as a young man made frequent pilgrimages to hear his famous playing and to learn from him, and the Dane Buxtehude, who held a similar post at Lübeck, is of still greater note, for he was not only a fine player but a composer of consequence.

DIETRICH (originally Diderik) BUXTEHUDE (born 1637) was one of the composers who made use of the hymn-tunes or chorales and saw that these melodies, besides being the noblest form of congregational church music, could be introduced also into more elaborate forms of composition. When people hear a tune they know and love they are helped by it to understand that part of the music which is new to them, and so the practice of taking a familiar tune as the basis of new compositions has always been very popular from the time when church composers wrote masses upon *L'homme armé* and other favourite tunes to the present day, when we often hear music of various kinds based on well-known folk-songs and dances (cf. also p. 48). But the chorale preludes for the organ which Buxtehude and other composers wrote had a peculiar fitness, for the chorale tunes belonged to the churches in which they were played, and their use would call to mind beautiful and appropriate ideas. Buxtehude was particularly energetic in developing church music beyond the limits of the ordinary congregational service, for he carried on at Lübeck a kind of sacred concert in the church, called *Abendmusik* (evening music), in which motets and cantatas were sung by a choir with other instruments beside the organ; he composed a great deal of valuable work of this kind which was an example to J. S. Bach later on.

### HARPSICHORD MUSIC

Outside the church, however, music did not progress so quickly. There was in Germany nothing comparable to the violin sonatas and concertos of Italy, or the harpsichord school of

Couperin and others in France. It is said, indeed, that Buxtehude attempted some suites in which 'the nature and character of the planets' were 'agreeably expressed', but this would seem to have been rather a quaint idea than a genuine piece of artistic expression. Pachelbel, one of the organists of the south of Germany who studied his art in Vienna, had written a number of variations and other pieces for the harpsichord, but nothing which remains of practical importance to modern music.

A very worthy man, Johann Kuhnau, who, in 1701, was appointed to the important post of Cantor at St. Thomas's School in Leipzig, the chief musical position in the town, realized how little German musicians had done to make music of this kind, and he set to work to write pieces for the harpsichord which he called sonatas. They differed from the sonatas of Domenico Scarlatti, which contained only a single movement, and were more like modern sonatas in that movements of various kinds were grouped together as in suites; but the movements were either quite independent ideas, worked out like those of D. Scarlatti, without reference to dance forms, or else they were written to illustrate a story. The most interesting of all are a set of six called 'Bible Sonatas'; they illustrate stories from the Old Testament, such as David and Goliath, the marriage of Jacob, and the campaigns of Gideon, and Kuhnau was particularly clever in finding musical phrases which would express the underlying ideas connected with the stories. For instance, he uses a heavy treading figure beginning deep down in the bass to suggest Goliath, which is rather like Wagner's theme for the giants in the *Rheingold*; again, the doubts of Gideon are suggested by phrases which first turn up and then down as though undecided what to do. Kuhnau tries to bring the whole story to the ears of his hearers, and sometimes he seems to imagine it performed on the stage, for he introduces passages almost like the recitatives and arias of opera. His musical descriptions are much more definite than those of Couperin, who liked to give character to his pieces by connecting them with fanciful ideas, but who did not always trouble to make the connexions clear to his audiences as Kuhnau did. If Kuhnau had had the opportunity he would certainly have left some remarkable contribution to German opera, but Leipzig offered none. Schütz's early introduction of opera at Torgau had made no permanent mark, and the only centre in Germany where opera took a firm hold at this time was Hamburg, which from its position in the extreme north could not much influence the musicians of Saxony.

At Hamburg, in the very end of the seventeenth century (1697), an opera house was opened by a remarkable composer named Reinhard Keiser, who, during the thirty years that followed, poured out one opera after another, producing alto-gether more than a hundred works of the kind. There is good reason to suppose that even J. S. Bach, who never wrote or wanted to write an opera, learnt a good deal from the fluent and varied arias of Keiser, and even copied their style in some of his cantatas; and since Handel came to Hamburg and first held a post in the orchestra of the theatre and produced his first opera there, Keiser's opera house certainly deserves to be remembered.

If you look up these towns on a map you will see how music was spreading through the centre of Germany at this time. The very fact that it could be illustrated by a map shows that the musical movement was far more widespread than in other countries. It would be absurd to draw a musical map of either France or England, for in those countries practically the whole of the musical culture was concentrated in the capitals, Paris and London. If we were to draw one of Italy it would be only necessary to put in half a dozen large towns. But in Germany music was spreading amongst the people of a great many small and little-known towns, and these people were not only practis-ing music but creating it, and that fact accounts for the enormous strength of German music in the next generation, since so many earnest men contributed splendid work in different departments. It only required some supreme genius to arise in order to sum up the different lines of effort in his own life-work, and it so happened that two such men were born in the same year, 1685, whose lives and work we must now study in detail, though one of them was to forsake the country of his birth and leave no traces of direct influence upon German music.

## *Suggestions for Further Reading and Listening*

IN the *New Oxford History of Music* the period of this chapter is covered, and more than covered, by vols. v and vi ('Opera and Church Music, 1630–1750' and 'The Growth of Instrumental Music, 1630–1750'); they will thus serve again at a later stage. Extensive articles will be found in Grove on opera, oratorio, Passion music, cantata, and sonata. Musical literature now becomes much richer in special studies of various subjects and of separate composers: a selection from the latter is here enumerated in the order in which they occur in the chapter.

On Alessandro Scarlatti Professor E. J. Dent's book is still valuable. It has long been out of print, but may be had from many libraries. On Corelli there is a chapter (shared with Vivaldi), by Philip Radcliffe, in vol. iii of *The Heritage of Music*, edited by Hubert Foss. The same author has an essay on both Alessandro and Domenico Scarlatti in vol. ii of that publication; but the important work on Domenico is that by Ralph Kirkpatrick. There is no English book on Lully, but Wilfrid Mellers's chapter in vol. iii of *The Heritage of Music* is excellent. An English translation of Paul Brunold's *François Couperin* was made by J. B. Hanson. Blow, Wise, and Locke are best studied in Grove in the first place, and further bibliographies of articles in various periodicals will be found there for the first and last. Purcell, as befits his greatness, is very much better served with books by J. A. Westrup ('Master Musicians' series), A. K. Holland (Penguin), Dennis Arundell, and a translation of a French work by Henry Dupré. For the German composers mentioned at the end of the chapter, apart from the two great masters who occupy the rest of this volume, Grove will have to serve again.

Something more may be learned about them through the gramophone. Vols. v–vi of *The History of Music in Sound* provide excellent examples of Keiser, Buxtehude, and Pachelbel. They also offer rich material for the Italian, French, and English sections of the chapter. Indeed, information on various masters not mentioned there may usefully be gleaned from the accompanying pamphlets. With the exception of Purcell and Domenico Scarlatti, and to a lesser extent Corelli, the composers who do occur in the chapter are very poorly represented by ordinary commercial recordings. They give no idea at all, for instance, of Lully and Rameau as operatic composers. But it is always worth while looking out for new publications, and meanwhile a splendid service has been rendered to Couperin by the Lyre-bird Press with the issue of a representative selection from his concerted instrumental and church music, issued in connexion with a collected edition of his works. Records of a number of his harpsichord pieces, indispensable for illustration, are also to be had.

# CHAPTER IV

## *The Lives of Handel and Bach*

HALLE in Saxony and Eisenach in Thuringia are only about eighty miles from each other as the crow flies. In the spring of the year 1685 these two small towns were in reality, though no one could guess it at the time, the mainsprings of the whole musical world, for in February Georg Friederich Händel was born at Halle, and a month later Johann Sebastian Bach was born at Eisenach.

From the first the circumstances of the lives of the two children were very different. Handel, as we will now call him, and as he came to call himself, the son of a barber-surgeon who made up his mind that his son must be a lawyer, not only had no encouragement to become a musician but was kept away from music by every means which the zealous father could devise. He could only learn to play by stealthily practising on a small clavichord which a kindhearted relative had hidden for his benefit in an attic. On the other hand, music was the natural way of life for every member of the Bach family, and that Johann Sebastian should be thoroughly educated in it as far as his father and brothers could teach it was a matter of course. This difference of circumstance no doubt helped to mould the characters of the two boys; Handel's determination to carve out a career for himself and to convince the world of his power, no matter what the odds against him might be, was strengthened; Bach's pure love of music for its own sake without regard for its effect upon others was expanded by the early conditions. A change very soon came in Handel's case, however, for he was only seven years old when the Duke of Saxe-Weissenfels persuaded the father to withdraw his objection to his son's music, and after this time he was at least given regular teaching, even though he could not find practical help or sympathy at home.

He was still torn between his own passionate desire to devote himself to music and his father's demand that he should study the law, and he seems to have made a really noble effort to fulfil both requirements even after his father's death in 1697; but at last the struggle had to be given up, and when he was eighteen years old he said good-bye to his mother at Halle and set out to seek his fortune in Hamburg which, as we have already seen, was the greatest musical centre of North Germany.

In the meantime Bach's difficulties had been of another order. He had lost both his parents by the time that he was ten, and after his father's death he had gone to live with an elder brother who was good to him but evidently ruled over him with a strictness which elder brothers are apt to show. For there is a story that Johann Sebastian, anxious to learn all about music, copied out by moonlight the contents of a precious manuscript which belonged to his brother, and when the brother discovered it he not only took away the original but the boy's copy too. In spite of such small restrictions, however, he had plenty of opportunity of learning until he was fifteen, when it was thought to be time for him to begin to make his own way in the world, and so he entered the choir of St. Michael's Church at Lüneburg. The organist was an intelligent man who had been acquainted with the great Schütz in Dresden, and he no doubt made Johann Sebastian know and love that composer's motets and Passion music. At Lüneburg there was another musician, Boehm, who had been a pupil of Reinken, and thus Bach became indirectly acquainted with the works of two great masters, the one of choral music, the other of the organ. Naturally he was fired with an ambition to hear Reinken play. Lüneburg, as you will see from the map, is not a great distance from Hamburg, and Bach walked to Hamburg on several occasions to hear all the music that he could, and especially to hear the great organist. The latest of these visits may even have taken place in the year 1703 when Handel also came to Hamburg, not as a student to hear and learn, but as a young musician whose first business was to find out how he might make a living. This difference of object was quite enough to account for the fact that the two never met, for Handel secured a post as violin player in the orchestra of Keiser's opera house, and if Bach visited the opera, as he probably did, it was to occupy a place on the back benches and listen. He never came in contact with the people connected with the opera, and at this time his chief love was certainly given to church and organ music.

This time formed the turning-point in the careers of both young men; it decided their different lines of action, lines which diverged so far from one another that no two contemporary composers seem less alike in thought and feeling than Handel and Bach. Handel became entirely wrapped up in the attractions of an operatic career. He rose from the poor position of a secondary fiddler to the important one of player on the harpsichord, which was equivalent to conducting in modern opera, and then in January 1705 came the great moment when an opera of his own composition was performed, and *Almira*, as it was called, was pronounced to be an unqualified success. The love of the stage and the ambition to write music for the theatre took possession of him and he longed to visit Italy, the land from which dramatic music had sprung and where it still flourished more abundantly than in Germany. He only waited to find the necessary funds to take him there; in the year after the production of *Almira* this difficulty was overcome and he started on his travels.

Long before this Bach's training at Lüneburg was over and he had returned to the district of Thuringia to take up a comparatively small organist's post at Arnstadt and to put into practice in his own playing some of the wonderful effects which he had heard Reinken use. He must have longed to see more of the world and to hear more music, and once he did break away from his narrow surroundings and travelled up to the north again to hear Buxtehude's music at Lübeck. When he was there he was so fascinated by all that he heard that he could not bring himself to go back to quiet little Arnstadt at the appointed time, and he got into trouble with the church people for playing truant so long. They also complained of his playing, because they could not understand the way in which he would improvise new harmonies to the chorales, and make long and elaborate preludes before the hymns. They wanted a commonplace parish church organist, not a great genius whose one thought was to make his art as perfect as possible. The incident is a sample of Bach's life. It was all spent in a few comparatively small places where he held honourable but more or less humble appointments. No one suspected that he was more than a clever player and a learned musician, or that the works which he played on his organ or wrote for his choir to sing would come to be considered as the greatest among musical works by musicians all the world over. The actual incidents of his life are important to us now only because the various appointments which he held influenced the music he wrote. For example, in these early days when he was organist first at Arnstadt, then at Mühlhausen, and finally at the court of the Duke of Saxe-Weimar, his mind was naturally filled with the possibilities of his instrument, and many of the great organ works such as the famous Prelude and Fugue in D major, and the Toccata and Fugue in D minor were written at Weimar, as well as some of the church cantatas. Then, when Bach became *Kapellmeister* to the Duke of Anhalt-Köthen (1717) he had an orchestra to train instead of a choir, and as he had no organ he naturally played more on his harpsichord and clavichord, and wrote music for them. After 1723, when he succeeded Kuhnau as Cantor of St. Thomas's School at Leipzig, he began to write choral music again, and from this time onward works of almost every kind flowed from his pen, innumerable cantatas, the Passion music, the oratorios, of which the *Christmas Oratorio* is the most famous, the Mass in B minor, and instrumental music chiefly for the organ or for his favourite little clavichord.

The names of Weimar, Köthen, and Leipzig, therefore, can be made to stand for the three stages of Bach's career; Weimar for the time when he poured out all his youthful ardour in the massive effects of the organ and began to feel his way towards the special style of church music which he perfected later; Köthen for his activity in other kinds of instrumental music, especially the concertos for various instruments, the sonatas for the violin, the suites for violoncello, and a great part of the clavichord music; Leipzig for the full expression of all his powers, especially in large church works which include both voices and instruments.

The rest of his story is merely a record of quiet home-life broken only by occasional visits to other towns for business or pleasure or for both, since Bach's work was the delight of his life. He never left Germany except for a trip to Carlsbad when he was *Kapellmeister* to Prince Leopold. A visit to Dresden when he was living at Weimar, and the famous one in his old age when his son Carl Philipp induced him to visit the court of Frederick the Great at Potsdam were almost the whole extent of Bach's travels after he settled down to continuous work. He married early, when he was only two and twenty, and the fact of having a wife to care for and a family of sons to educate was another circumstance which kept him from moving far or indulging in large schemes such as occupied Handel's life. His first wife died just when the elder children were growing up and when the eldest son's talent for music was beginning to show itself. Bach had written a book of clavier pieces to teach this boy, Wilhelm Friedemann, in the same year that his wife, Maria Barbara, died at Köthen (1720). In the following year he was married again to Anna Magdalena Wilcken, who was evidently very musical, for soon after their marriage he wrote pieces and songs for her to sing and play, and throughout the years of their married life together at Leipzig, when Bach had to teach his boys at St. Thomas's School and superintend the music of no less than four churches, she helped him greatly in his busy life by copying out his music for performance.

We left Handel setting off for Italy in 1706 at about the time when Bach made the last of his youthful pilgrimages to visit Buxtehude. Bach could be scolded by churchwardens of limited imagination for staying away more than a certain time, but Handel was a free man. He was not bound by any times or appointments; he had saved sufficient money to make him independent for some time to come, he had made enough friends in Hamburg to secure him an introduction into the artistic circles of Italy, and although he was only twenty-one years old he had gained a reputation by his playing and by his composition, which made even the Italians respect him, though in general they were apt to think that no one but themselves knew anything at all about music. Handel was in fact most kindly treated by the Italians, by the wealthy patrons of art, by the musicians like the Scarlattis and Corelli, who made friends with him in Rome (see p. 57), and by the general public, who cheered him to the echo when his opera *Agrippina* was performed at Venice. Handel went from one place to another astonishing people by his powers, and yet he did not forget that he had come to Italy chiefly to learn. He certainly studied the music of the Italians very closely, for his own style became very like theirs. In his later operas and oratorios one can trace very clearly the influence of Scarlatti and even of Carissimi (though the latter was long since dead), while his later instrumental works are directly founded upon the style of Corelli (see p. 131). Altogether Handel's visit to Italy lasted until 1709. In spite of his success he seems to have had no thought of settling down to the life of an Italian opera composer in Italy itself. Probably he felt that the country was too crowded with musicians. He wanted to find a fresh field for himself, and possibly he thought that he would find such an opportunity in his own country. So in 1710 he accepted the post of *Kapellmeister* to the Elector of Hanover, and scarcely had he done so than he began to feel restless.

The court at Hanover was very unlike the brilliant courts of Italian princes. There was no chance of its providing any great occasion for a musician like Handel; there was no opera house to write for; there was nothing but a dreary round of services in the Protestant chapel, and small music-makings for the entertainment of the Elector and the court. Handel was not a man like Bach who could do great work in the most uninspiring conditions. He required the incentive of great opportunities, but he would not sit quiet and wait for great opportunities to come. If they did not come in Hanover he would go and seek them elsewhere. He had met some Englishmen in Italy and he had been pressed to visit London. He made up his mind to give London a trial, and so having obtained leave of absence from the Elector he came there in the autumn of 1710.

By this time the wave of musical enthusiasm which had filled London after the Restoration had dwindled down. Purcell had been dead for fifteen years, and with him had died the chance of any distinctive form of English dramatic music. Even John Blow, whose influence upon music outside the church was never very strong, was now dead. A few Italian operas had been tried in London just as at an earlier time Italian operas were tried in Paris before Lully took command of Parisian music. Now London required someone to take command, and Handel was certainly the man to do it. Not that he could do at the court of Queen Anne what Lully did at the court of Louis XIV. He could not wait and watch and find out what would please; it was not his nature to do so. On the contrary, he had spent his younger years in learning every detail of one kind of art, the Italian opera, and that was what he had to offer to the English. He did not come to consult their tastes or to find out what they had been used to in the stage music of their own country. If they liked what he gave them well and good, if not he would go back to Hanover. He had powerful friends who could arrange for the production of his operas in London, and he instantly set to work and wrote *Rinaldo*, which was first performed in the spring of the next year (1711).

*Rinaldo* was a version of the story of *Armida*, which we described in connexion with Lully's opera. It is recorded that the whole play was gorgeously put upon the stage and that everything that scenery and stage mechanism could do to make it effective was done, even to the flight of hundreds of birds on the stage in the scene of the enchanted garden. Whether because of these trivial details or because the English audience had never heard songs of such sustained power, beauty, and variety as Handel wrote, the result was a complete success, and Handel realized that London was his great opportunity. He had to go back to his duties at Hanover, however, but he evidently went with the determination to spend as little time there as possible, for in 1712 he was back in London again. Though he had only leave to come for a short time he soon got so involved in London life that he never went back to stay at Hanover. Meantime, he began to work with a most remarkable man named Heidegger, who was famous as a stage-manager and almost equally famous for his own personal ugliness. It seemed at first as if Handel were to continue through his life the brilliant success which he had met with everywhere, in Hamburg, in Italy, and in London. For not only was his new opera *Teseo* well received, but he began to be counted as the foremost man in London music. When the peace of Utrecht was proclaimed in 1713 Handel was invited to write the 'Te Deum' which was sung as a national thanksgiving, and after this the Queen granted him a small pension. With the Queen's death (1714) Handel's popularity received its first check, for the Elector of Hanover, whom he had really treated rather badly, came to England as King George I, and let it be seen that his *Kapellmeister* was in disgrace and that he had no business to be here. George, indeed, heard one of Handel's operas, but still ignored the composer, and it was not until Handel had composed the famous 'Water Music' to entertain the King on the river that he was taken back into favour, if the rather uncertain story is to be believed. He had to do penance by going back to Hanover with George and his suite in 1716, but after this one visit he was not troubled with Hanover any more. England became his home, and in future he only left it to make rapid tours either to Dresden or to Italy in order to engage opera singers, or to recover his health when he had been overworked.

Nevertheless, the apparent settlement of difficulties was really the beginning of Handel's troubles. From 1717 onward he settled down to his curious work of planting Italian opera in English soil. People sometimes speak and write as though Handel made the Italian operas to please the society people of London and English oratorios to satisfy his own ideals. This is quite untrue. Handel believed absolutely in the future of Italian opera. He went on in the face of every obstacle trying to make it thrive. The society people cared not one jot for the drama as expressed in music; nor could most of them understand Italian or appreciate great art when they heard it. All the majority cared for was to patronize one composer at the expense of another or to back one popular singer against another. Handel had to meet all the difficulties of keeping a company together, of persuading or more often compelling foolish singers to sing his music in a reasonable way, of reconciling the quarrels of rival singers, of competing with other operatic ventures which were started merely in order to injure him. If we were studying the history of Handel rather than the history of music we should have to tell the whole story in detail. As it is we need only say that an institution called the Royal Academy of Music was started in 1719, chiefly by the King and his household, for the production of Italian opera, and for this Handel worked assiduously for several years, producing one work after another. When it failed in 1727 Handel started a venture on his own account with his old colleague Heidegger, and struggled on through ten more years trying to convince people that there was more in opera than only singing and scenery. His antagonists (a rival opera house had been started by certain of the nobility) were too strong for him, that is to say, they ruined themselves and him too by their futile competition. Handel was broken down in fortune and in health in the summer of 1737, though never actually bankrupt, but in that autumn he returned to the charge and for several years afterwards he risked operatic ventures, though by this time he was finding out the capacities of oratorio as a means both of expressing himself and of suiting the more genuine taste of the English public.

During the early years of his career in England Handel had

plenty of inducements to leave opera for other forms of musical work. The Duke of Chandos, who lived in greater state than any other noble of the time, appointed him to be his chapel master on the same plan as that of the German rulers who kept musicians to supply them with music. The Duke had a large house with a private chapel at Canons Park, near Edgware; when Handel became a member of his household in 1718 he had enough to do to keep any ordinary man busy. But although he wrote some fine church music, now known as the Chandos Anthems, and produced *Esther* for the Duke's entertainment, he could not long be kept from his operatic efforts.

*Esther* was a kind of play founded upon the Biblical story of Queen Esther and King Ahasuerus. The music was set to English words, and Handel at first called it a 'masque', and intended it to be acted on the stage at the Duke's private house, just as the old English masques of Lawes and others had been acted (see pp. 46–47 and 81). *Esther* was simply a dramatic offshoot, and it was not until many years after, when Handel had written most of his best operas, when the Royal Academy of Music had failed and he was hard pressed to hold his own against the opera house of the nobility, that it occurred to him that music of this kind might be made genuinely popular.

In the year 1732 the choir-boys of the Chapel Royal got up a private performance of Handel's masque of *Esther*, and acted it in the presence of Handel himself and a small but distinguished audience. It pleased people so much that it had to be repeated in public, but since the Bishop of London objected to the practice of acting a biblical play in a theatre, it had to be given without stage action. He also rewrote an earlier work of his called *Acis and Galatea*, and gave it in the theatre with appropriate scenery, but without any action on the stage. In the following year in Lent, when the performance of opera was thought to be unsuitable, Handel made fresh attempts in this new kind of entertainment, half theatrical, half biblical. He used other Old Testament subjects, such as *Deborah* and *Athaliah*, evidently because their stories included great and stirring events which could be vividly illustrated in music. Though he had to give up the scenic effects of opera, the loss was more than balanced by the fact that he could make much greater use of the chorus and so gain massive musical effects which were out of the question on the stage (see p. 51). The new form gradually grew on Handel's imagination, and year by year he produced further works of the kind, which, with very few exceptions, such as *Israel in Egypt* and *Messiah*, are really operas in disguise, for their librettos contain no narratives and their plots are shown in direct action. The choruses, it is true, often provide comments, but so do those in ancient Greek tragedy. Handel also revived the performance of choral odes which had been so popular in Purcell's day (see pp. 79–81). In 1736 he set Dryden's ode, *Alexander's Feast*, to music, and in 1739 he set Dryden's *Ode on St. Cecilia's Day*, in which he actually seems to have copied Purcell's style to some extent.

*Saul* and *Israel in Egypt* appeared in the same year, 1738. *Messiah* was given first at Dublin in 1742, where Handel had been asked to go by the Lord Lieutenant of Ireland, and it and *Samson* were produced in London in the following season. The year 1745, when the Jacobite rising in Scotland had been suppressed by the battle of Culloden, was celebrated by the production of *Judas Maccabaeus*, of which the chief themes are war, bloodshed, and military glory; from this time until the end of his life Handel and his oratorio performances seem to have become a recognized part of London life, and he was able to carry them on regularly and successfully almost up to the time of his death in 1759.

Bach had died in Leipzig nine years earlier (1750). The two had never met, though once, when Handel had been paying a visit to his mother at Halle, Bach had made a special journey from Köthen in the hope of meeting him. But he had come too late. Though Bach stayed at home he was in close touch with the music of other countries, for he never lost an opportunity of studying such of it as was published. Handel's fame was very great, and probably Bach knew a good deal of his work, but on the other hand Bach can have been known to Handel only as a fine organist who had written some music. Very little of Bach's work was published during his lifetime, and that his reputation was local is shown by the fact that after his death his great choral works were laid aside and forgotten for nearly a hundred years.

## *Suggestions for Further Reading and Listening*

FURTHER reading in connexion with this chapter will as a matter of course be mainly biographical. Where this book is being used in class illustration with the aid of the gramophone will perhaps be deferred by the teacher until the following chapter is reached. But there is no reason why the stories of Handel's and Bach's careers should not be enlivened by specimens of their work where they happen to fit in. Passages played on the piano, or even short records, will break up the narrative both agreeably and instructively where it relates the circumstances surrounding some particular work, such as the music-book compiled by Bach for his second wife, Anna Magdalena, or Handel's 'Water Music'. The teacher may also care to enlarge on the influence of some composers dealt with in Chapter III on the two masters by playing suitable specimens side by side: e.g. an aria by Alessandro Scarlatti and one by Handel, parts of the latter's Utrecht 'Te Deum' and of Purcell's Te Deum and Jubilate, or a dance piece by one of the French clavecinists and one from Bach's clavier suites resembling it in style.

The biographical literature is abundant, even in English alone, and excluding (for the purpose of the present chapter) works concerned only with the study of Bach's and Handel's music. The great standard biography of Bach actually written in English is that by Charles Sanford Terry. German works translated before its appearance include that by Johann Nikolaus Forkel—the earliest of all—that by Philipp Spitta, and that by Albert Schweitzer. A shorter work, by Eva Mary and Sydney Grew ('Master Musicians' series), though not sufficiently comprehensive on the music, deals with the life satisfactorily in a small space. Of these books only Terry and Forkel are purely biographical: the others will concern us again later.

A very early work on Handel, J. Mainwaring's *Memoirs*, which appeared in 1760, the year after the master's death, has formed a basis for most of the later biographies. Another standard work was Victor Schoelcher's, published nearly a century later, in 1857. Both have called for some correction in various details. The largest modern biography in English is that by Newman Flower. Quite short, but full of interesting and original observation is Edward J. Dent's volume in the 'Great Lives' series. The contribution to the 'Master Musicians' series is a more sizable work by Percy M. Young. A large volume, for reference rather than continuous reading, containing a complete collection of biographical raw material, is Otto Erich Deutsch's *Handel: a Documentary Biography*.

The choice of gramophone records, as has already been suggested, must necessarily be rather capricious for this chapter. Each reader will no doubt decide what is best, performance being here very largely dependent on individual extensions of the text. The few suggestions made above and hereafter, on the other hand, can only keep close to it. It may be thought desirable to go back to Heinrich Schütz, although he was born a hundred years before Bach and Handel, as a great master and here mentioned for such slight influence as he had on Bach. Some of that master's music alluded to on p. 96 may perhaps be listened to in short specimens, though it will all become more relevant later on. Organ and chamber music will be most suitable here. Handel's *Acis and Galatea* and *Alexander's Feast* will yield something for pp. 102–3, but the familiar oratorios had better be deferred, as they will become especially useful for the next chapter.

# CHAPTER V

# Vocal Music of Handel and Bach

## HANDEL'S OPERATIC STYLE

I N all probability you will never have an opportunity of hearing an opera by Handel. He adopted the formal style of the Italians so completely that a modern performance can be attempted only in special circumstances for its historical interest. A vast amount of glorious music is thus wasted, but a style of opera in which there must be always six principal characters, each one of which must sing a certain number of arias in certain fixed styles and leave the stage at the conclusion of each, whatever the dramatic situation, is a kind of entertainment very difficult to revive. Each aria was complete in itself, and was generally worked out fully according to the ternary *da capo* form which Scarlatti had made fashionable (see p. 55), so that there could be no real progress of the drama in the course of an aria, since the singer had always to return to the point from which he started. Occasionally a piece of fine recitative would break through the monotonous scheme, and now and then a chorus was introduced, as at the beginning of *Giulio Cesare*, when the composer wished to gain a particularly impressive effect from the scene of Julius Caesar's camp on the Egyptian plains. Such departures are rare, however, and do very little to break the general rule.

Yet for half his life Handel put the best of his energies into composing operas of this kind, and they are full of splendidly free and flowing melodies, some of which you may hear in concert rooms, though many of the best of them are quite forgotten. A few are so well known that you may easily remember the operas in which they occur by means of them. 'Lascia ch'io pianga' is often played and sung, though most often with altered English words, and comes from his first opera in England, *Rinaldo*. The famous march from *Scipione*, which Gay introduced into *The Beggar's Opera* ('Let us take the road') will serve to remind you of one of the most famous operas of the Royal Academy period, and the lovely melody of 'Ombra mai fù', which for some reason is more often known as 'Handel's Largo'—as though he had not marked innumerable slow tunes of the same kind to be played *largo* (e.g. slowly)—comes from *Serse* (Xerxes), one of the latest operas (1738), produced with Heidegger after Handel had already begun to rely more on his oratorios as a means of reaching success.

Though you are not likely to gain a much closer knowledge of Handel's operas than a mere handful of the songs can give you, they have a great importance in musical history which has been too often forgotten. The long years of writing for the stage fixed Handel's method as that of a dramatic composer. Whenever he approached a subject, whether it was that of an opera, or an oratorio, or even that of a cantata like *Alexander's Feast*, it presented first to his mind a picture or series of pictures such as the stage produces to the eye. He saw before him the scene which the subject represented; he felt all the sensations which the events of the story would produce upon the minds of the people concerned in it, and his aim was to make his music convey the scene, the events, and the feelings of the people to his audience so that they might share them too. His famous exclamation about the Hallelujah chorus, 'I did think I did see Heaven opened and the great God himself', shows that even *Messiah*, which is less like his opera form than any one of the oratorios, was based to some extent upon a dramatic mental picture, though the picture in his mind's eye was the most sublime one possible.

## HANDEL'S ATTITUDE TOWARDS ORATORIO

Many parts of the oratorios are simply operatic scenes upon Old Testament subjects, but the presence of a large chorus to take the place of the stage was a new factor which gradually led him away from the attitude of direct representation to a more reflective one. It will be easier to understand this if we look closely at one of his most representative oratorios, *Saul*.

After the overture the oratorio opens with a massive chorus, 'How excellent is Thy name', in which the Jewish people praise God for David's victory over Goliath. For this Handel used a particularly big orchestra in which trombones, trumpets, and drums were added to the more usual instruments, and it is quite evident that his main object was to present a scene of national rejoicing. A short soprano air exults in the prowess of David, and then 'the monster atheist' is described in a short trio, the orchestral music of which suggests his big and lumbering form by repeating a heavy unison phrase (cf. Kuhnau, p. 89). Another chorus tells in a bold theme how the courage of the Israelites was restored by the sight of Goliath overthrown, and how they 'headlong drove that impious crew', and then the chorus bursts into a repetition of the first hymn of praise and ends the scene with a ringing chorus of Hallelujahs.

The scene is dramatic, but it is not operatic, for it contemplates the story of David and Goliath, and does not try to give a direct representation of it. The following scenes of the oratorio are carried on in a strictly operatic way. All the principal characters make their appearance in turn. First comes Michal, the daughter of Saul, who loves David and sings a song in his praise. Then Abner, the captain of the host, presents David to Saul who promises him the hand of his elder daughter Merab in marriage. Merab, however, despises him, and sings a very vigorous song to describe her emotions; finally comes Jonathan, who greets David with friendship in music of a calmer kind than that given to most of the characters. Then a chorus of maidens, accompanied by a carillon (that is a peal of bells played from a keyboard), enters with the song 'Saul has slain his thousands and David his ten thousands', which rouses Saul's bitter jealousy. The well-known story of the evil spirit taking possession of Saul, of David's playing before him, and his attempt to kill David is told with characteristic songs and recitatives, and there is a harp solo to represent David's performance;

it is just as though the characters were enacting the whole before our eyes upon a stage. So much is this the case that Handel never troubles to tell his audience that Saul threw a javelin at David. He merely makes Saul sing an aria of burning hate and rage, and a rapid scale of demi-semi-quavers on the strings is meant to indicate the flight of the javelin, as though the composer were so completely wrapped up in the picture before his eyes that he had forgotten that the audience would not see it acted as he did in imagination. It is not until the very end of the first part that Handel seems to remember that after all his work is not an opera, for he then finishes off the part with a chorus which is not actually a part of the story but rather a comment on it.

The events of the second part of Saul are much less stirring than those of the first. The temporary reconciliation between Saul and David, the marriage of David with Michal, Saul's attempt to kill Jonathan, do not call out the same dramatic power or pictorial brilliancy which Handel bestowed on the first part. The marriage scene is passed over with a short love duet, and a conventional chorus follows to point the moral that love is superior to hatred. Handel seems less inspired by this part of his subject, although the opening chorus, 'Envy, eldest born of hell', is as bold and original as any number in the whole work, and the final chorus, 'O fatal consequence of rage', is another fine number. The events, and still more the emotions underlying the events of the third part, however, seized upon Handel's vivid imagination as forcibly as did those of the first part. Saul's visit to the Witch of Endor is treated most graphically. The witch's invocation is made to sound strange and unearthly by the violins playing a figure which continually falls and rises again by large intervals, and the hollow tones of the bassoons carry on the same feeling into the solemn recitative in which the spirit of Samuel speaks to Saul.

A very short orchestral interlude joins this to the scene after the battle when the Amalekite comes to tell David of the death of Saul. In a short but powerful song David condemns him for slaying the Lord's Anointed, and then follows the wonderful Dead March, which has become one of the most celebrated pieces in the whole range of music connected with the subject of death. After this the course of the oratorio turns completely away from anything like dramatic action until the end, when David is hailed as king by the people.

Immediately after the Dead March comes the lament for Saul and Jonathan, the point which shows us most clearly the difference between true oratorio, i.e. musical comment upon a dramatic subject, and opera, which is the direct representation of a drama in music. Handel carries it on by means of the chorus alternating with the solo voice of David. It begins with a beautiful choral number, 'Mourn Israel'. Then a recitative, 'O let it not in Gath be heard', is followed by arias, and a short chorus, 'Eagles were not so swift as they', made vivid by the rushing scales of the violins and the bass part moving continuously in rapid quavers. More arias and a fine number, 'O fatal day', in which both the solo and the chorus take part, continue the lament and lead up to the most imposing chorus in the oratorio, 'Gird on thy sword', which makes an inspiring climax.

This examination of *Saul* has shown us that almost everywhere the use of the chorus tends to make the oratorio less directly theatrical in style. There are some exceptions. The chorus of maidens singing the praise of David in the first part is one of them, for the maidens belong to the action of the story, and their music might be sung and danced to on the stage with even better effect than it has on the concert platform. But elsewhere it is in the great reflective parts, especially in the lament and the finale, that the chorus is most powerful. Handel realized this, and in the same year that he wrote *Saul* he produced *Israel in Egypt*, which practically is made up of indirect reflection upon the dramatic situation by means of huge choral numbers.

The first part of *Israel in Egypt*, dealing with the plagues of Egypt and the passage of the Israelites through the Red Sea, shows Handel's power of writing vivid descriptive music more than any other work, in spite of the fact that he used a good deal of his own and other people's earlier music as material for it. The second part, the song of praise for the delivery out of Egypt, is on a much larger scale, like the lament which is the culminating point of *Saul*, except that it is a song of joy instead of one of sorrow. It does not tell a story, but it dwells in an heroic style upon the great events which are past and the feelings of triumphant thankfulness which they call up. This is really the true business of oratorio, for it can never picture actions as well as opera can, but it can express the underlying thoughts and ideas far more thoroughly.

The mixture, however, of the direct, operatic style with the reflective one of oratorio is found in almost all Handel's works of the kind, and you may distinguish the two very clearly in *Samson*, *Judas Maccabaeus*, *Solomon*, and *Jephthah*, all of which were later than *Israel*. In only one of the works which follow *Israel* did he abandon the operatic manner altogether, and that was in the only Christian oratorio which he ever wrote, *Messiah*.

In *Messiah* he made no attempt to give a dramatic representation of the birth, life, and passion of the Saviour, and only in one instance, in the scene of the angels appearing to the shepherds of Bethlehem, did he give a description of events. He used both solo voices and chorus as a means of meditating upon the facts of the story, and consequently recitative, which was his usual means of relating incidents or conversations between the principal characters, is reduced to a minimum. It is partly because the subject is so much greater than the semi-barbaric stories which he usually set to music, and partly because it is so much more truly fitted to the method of oratorio, that *Messiah* has been judged universally to be Handel's greatest work. We may find choruses in the other oratorios which are finer than 'For unto us' or 'His yoke is easy', and solos which surpass 'Rejoice greatly' or 'Why do the heathen', but no oratorio is so consistent in aim as *Messiah*. His own remark about the 'Hallelujah' chorus shows that his strong dramatic sense guided his choice of a subject and directed his effects, but he had thrown off theatrical means of expression entirely, and

nore upon the deeper meaning and the emotions
  the subject than upon its external features. *Messiah*
  uggests a comparison with Bach's great choral works
  ne subject, but before we can make such a comparison
  ssary to trace the growth of Bach's work in much the
same way as we have traced that of Handel.

### BACH'S CHURCH CANTATAS

Bach's style grew out of the church music of his own country
just as Handel's grew out of Italian opera. We have seen that
the basis of Lutheran church music was the hymn-tune or
chorale, and that composers both in writing for instruments
and for voices in church cantatas (which took the place of the
anthems of the Anglican church) used both tunes and words of
chorales as their groundwork (see p. 88). Bach followed their
example in this as in other features of his work, but in the course
of his life he borrowed ideas from many sources, and even
incorporated some of the principles which Scarlatti and the
Italians had discovered.

No sooner had Bach settled down to his life as a church
organist than he began to compose cantatas which could take
their places in the services of his church. Among those composed at Weimar is the beautiful one, *Gottes Zeit ist die allerbeste
Zeit* ('God's time is ever the best time'), which gives a wonderful picture of the point from which Bach started. A very short
instrumental movement written for two flutes, two *viole da
gamba*, and basses with organ opens the work, and is described
as a 'Sonata', though it is unlike any of the sonata forms of the
day. It is followed by a chorus on these words:

> God's time is ever the best time.
> In Him we live and move and have our being
> So long as He wills.
> In Him we die at the right time when He wills,

which sets the subject for meditation. A composer who had not
Bach's keen sense of what is beautiful and appropriate in music

would have dropped into writing music which merely set forth
the words without adding anything to the force of the idea.
But Bach's mind was of a kind which saw the inner meaning
underlying the conventional expression, and could make every
feature of his music, the rise and fall of his melody, the rhythm
and the harmony correspond closely to some phase of that
meaning. For example, in this cantata the first chorus is full of
confidence. Both its themes are made of strong rising figures:

Ex. 26

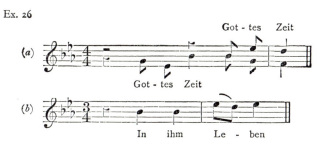

and he reserves more intimate expression for the numbers which
follow. The words for these are drawn from various texts of
the Bible. First, a tenor solo prays 'O Lord, teach us to number
our days', and a bass solo answers 'Set thine house in order for
thou shalt die and not live'. Then a remarkable chorus is sung
by the three lower voices (alto, tenor, and bass), 'It is the
ancient law; man thou must die', in which the music marches
forward with a relentless tread, and at the end the trebles sing
'Yea come, Lord Jesus come' to an infinitely touching phrase
which suggests the joyful acceptance of death by the Christian
soul. An alto voice sings the psalmist's words 'Into Thy hand
I commend my spirit', and a bass voice responds with those of
Christ on the Cross 'Today shalt thou be with me in Paradise'.
The way in which the bass voice breaks in with a sweeping
downward phrase on these words is specially noticeable, and
the reply of the alto singing a well-known chorale tune is very
beautiful. The last chorus of praise is also built on a chorale,
but it is very much ornamented both by the instrumental

accompaniment and by the ending in which the voices expand into rich polyphony.

Soon after writing this cantata Bach came across various collections of sacred poetry, from which he drew the words for many of his later works of the kind. In setting poetry he developed his arias more fully than in the earlier biblical cantatas, and very frequently made use of the ternary form which Scarlatti and the Italians had devised for their operas. But in whatever form he worked, the actual music which Bach wrote was much more deeply thoughtful than that of the Italians; his melodies were more original, his harmonies were more striking, and his skill in weaving the voice part together with independent instrumental parts was a most remarkable feature of his solo writing.

For the choruses he adopted a great number of different designs. Sometimes he would write free contrapuntal choruses or fugues, such as the first chorus of 'O ewiges Feuer' ('O Light everlasting'), but very often they were founded on chorales. The two late cantatas 'Wachet auf' ('Sleepers, wake'), and 'Ein' feste Burg' ('A stronghold sure'), show the different ways of treating the chorale most perfectly. The first is a setting of a fine Advent hymn by Dr. Philipp Nicolai; in the first chorus the words are sung by the treble to the traditional tune in its simple form, while the other voices sing all kinds of free melodies in conjunction with it. In the other, a setting of Luther's popular hymn, the tune is treated as though it were a fugue subject, and all the voices take part in singing fragments of it in turn, and a tremendous effect of polyphonic sound is built upon it (see pp. 144–6, chorales for organ). The tunes, too, are used in the solos and duets of these cantatas. In fact, Bach used every device which could illustrate his subjects most fully. The subjects themselves of the cantatas are very varied, but generally are suggested by the thoughts put forward by the Sundays of the ecclesiastical year. Sometimes they touch upon incidents in Bible stories; for example, 'Bleib' bei uns' ('Abide with us'), which takes as its subject the scene of the disciples at Emmaus;

they do not attempt to tell a story but rather to meditate upon the ideas it suggests.

## PASSION MUSIC

When we come to examine the large choral works by which Bach is best known, the two settings of the Passion, according to St. John and to St. Matthew, and *The Christmas Oratorio*, we find that the story takes a far more prominent place than in the cantatas, and that consequently they come very near to the kind of dramatic expression which was the life of Handel's oratorios. This is natural in the Passion, for the traditional object of Passion music was to recount the events of the Saviour's death, and however much it might be surrounded with other music which meditated upon the underlying thought, such ideas could never be allowed to obscure the story itself. In the Passions Bach secured the prominence of the story by setting aside one voice (a tenor) to sing all the words of the Gospel in recitative, with the exception of such parts as belong to conversations. A bass voice sang the words of the Saviour, and other individual voices were allotted to the words of Pilate, Peter, the High Priest, the witnesses, and others, while for any words which were originally spoken by a group of people (e.g. all the disciples together or the crowd who thronged into the Judgement Court) he used the whole chorus. This was the extension of the Roman Catholic plan adopted by Schütz (see p. 87). But Bach entered so much more deeply into the feelings of all those who took part in the tragedy of Calvary, and he had such a power of expressing himself in musical terms, that this part of the Passion music became a far more living thing than it had ever been before.

The *St. John Passion* shows him to some extent still feeling his way in this respect. The recitative is apt to repeat more conventional phrases than that of the *St. Matthew Passion*. The choruses representing the crowd are rather long and consequently not always very graphic. The scene of Peter's denial, however, is as perfectly carried out as anything in the later work. A recitative tells how Peter stood warming himself, and a little turn of four notes on the word 'warmed' suggests an attitude of affected carelessness. Then a short chorus of detached phrases makes a vivid picture of the chattering servants who accuse him of being one of the disciples of Jesus. Peter jerks out his denial with an evident effort in a phrase of three notes:

Ex. 27

I        am    not.

Then the cock crows : a little arpeggio on the violoncellos suggests its distant sounds. Peter remembers the words of Jesus, and his bitter weeping is described by the voice of the Evangelist in a long chromatic phrase in which all the pent-up feeling of the earlier part seems to burst forth in an agonized wail. No more perfect picture of weak human nature exists in music.

But while this scene is unsurpassable in the *St. John Passion* practically the whole of the narrative part of the *St. Matthew* is equally subtle. If the Passion music proper, according to St. Matthew, were performed without any of the chorales, songs, or choruses which comment upon it, it would sound like a wonderful sacred drama in music. Bach generally accompanied his recitative with the organ or harpsichord and merely the bass instruments in detached chords, but in the *St. Matthew Passion*, wherever the Saviour speaks, his words are accompanied by long sustained chords played by all the stringed instruments. They seem to surround his words with a reverent atmosphere like the halo of light which the old painters crowned their sacred figures. Throughout, the different characters are kept quite distinct. There is a serene dignity in every phrase of the music which belongs to the Saviour, and at times, more especially in the institution of the Sacrament, the recitative rises to the height of pure melody. When Judas speaks, it is generally in a phrase of rather harsh outline; Peter's short sentences in the denial are bolder than in the earlier Passion, and all the minor characters, the maid-servants, the glib false witnesses, even Pilate's wife, are carefully touched in. The choruses, too, are very graphic, from the frightened, questioning one in which the disciples ask who will betray their Master to the horrible clamour of the crowd 'Let Him be crucified', or the savage outburst of the single word 'Barrabas' which comes in answer to Pilate's question, 'Which then shall I release unto you?'

On the other hand, Bach continually broke through the progress of the Passion story to dwell in thought upon the meaning that each feature of it must have for the Christian. Sometimes he did this with a chorale in which all the congregation could take part. Very often he did it by means of a solo aria, generally when the incident on which it comments calls up intimate, personal feeling, such as the story of the penitent woman who bathed the feet of the Saviour, or the sorrow of Peter which calls forth the aria 'Have mercy Lord on me'. Occasionally the whole chorus has to be used to express the strongest emotions; for example, after the Saviour has been taken prisoner the two choirs burst out into a chorus of indignation at the outrage.

Both the Passions are begun with great choruses which take the place of the instrumental overtures to oratorios, and each ends with a wonderful choral lament which sums up the feeling in the most complete way.

### THE CHRISTMAS ORATORIO

We see, then, that in the Passions Bach kept two lines of thought and feeling continually present, the one dramatic, the other reflective. In the earlier parts of *The Christmas Oratorio* he did the same, for the story of the birth of Christ at Bethlehem, of the angels and the shepherds, is told in the same way by a tenor voice representing the Evangelist, and the angelic chorus 'Glory to God' is among his finest inspirations. But the story itself does not take the commanding position which that of the Passion does, and the later parts of *The Christmas Oratorio*, intended to be sung on the various festivals following Christmas day, are more like the cantatas. The story is merely the text for religious contemplation.

*The Christmas Oratorio* contains some specially remarkable numbers. For example, in the first part after the Evangelist has told of the birth of the Saviour 'Wrapped in swaddling clothes and laid in a manger', there is a duet in which bass recitative is combined with a chorale sung by treble voices. The trebles sing one phrase of the tune 'For us to earth He cometh poor', holding on the last note in a thoughtful way till the bass solo breaks in with the words,

> Who rightly can the love declare
> That fills our tender Saviour's breast,

and each phrase of the chorale calls out some fresh idea on which the recitative comments. Moreover, the whole is bound together into a perfect musical shape by the delicate instrumental music written for oboes and strings. Another is the lullaby sung by an alto voice, 'Slumber Beloved', one of the purest melodies Bach ever wrote, which, like several others, appeared originally in a secular cantata.

In the fourth part there is a treble song in which a second voice is made to reply in the manner of an echo, a quaint device which reminds one of some of the devotional poems of George Herbert, and in the fifth part a trio for treble, alto, and tenor represents a kind of movement which is very characteristic of Bach. The treble and tenor sing a melody full of ardent longing to the words 'Ah when shall we see salvation', and at the end of each musical sentence the alto stills their agitation with the words 'Peace, for surely this is He', set to quieter music. Bach had a special fondness for this kind of dialogue in music, and in several cantatas he introduced them to portray the communion between the soul and its Saviour.

### HANDEL AND BACH COMPARED

A comparison of the Shepherd scenes in Handel's *Messiah* and in Bach's *Christmas Oratorio* will show us the differences in the

thought and in the workmanship of the two composers. Ea
begins with a 'Pastoral Symphony', a piece of instrumental
music of a peaceful kind supposed to represent the scene of the
quiet countryside with the shepherds encamped upon the hill
making music to beguile their watch.

Handel's is written for string orchestra only; its simple
melody and artless style, the violin parts moving together
chiefly in thirds, gives just the right suggestion and nothing
more. Bach's is much more intricate. Oboes, flutes, and violins
weave a wonderful pattern of picturesque sound; two themes
are contrasted and combined, and the whole is worked out at
much greater length. We may leave out of count the chorales
and arias interspersed in Bach's work, and look only at the telling of the story which both have in common. In each case this
is done with recitative. The two settings of the words 'And lo!
the angel of the Lord came upon them, and the glory of the
Lord shone round about them and they were sore afraid', shows
all the different character of the two composers. Handel ac-
companies his with an excited figure for the violins which em-
phasizes the idea of the sudden light flooding in upon the dark-
ness. Bach attempts no such picture, but a long downward
phrase on the violoncellos makes one realize the fear of the
shepherds very forcibly. Again, we see Handel's love of pictorial effect in the recitative and chorus 'And suddenly there
was with the angel'. It is accompanied by a fluttering figure
for the violins which suggests the innumerable wings of the
heavenly host, and the chorus 'Glory to God' begins with
the three higher voices only, as though he wished to give a
feeling of sound gradually coming from the heights down to
earth.

We have seen that Bach, too, could use realistic effects (see
*St. John Passion*, p. 116), but he avoids them here. His recitative
is studiously simple, and he saves all his forces for a glorious
outburst of contrapuntal sound in the great chorus 'Glory to
God'. If we place these two choruses side by side, Handel's
seems small and almost trivial in comparison with the huge

and which Bach produces. But Handel's is really effective. It needs a skilled musician to hear all the ..ch's chorus; a child can distinguish everything in Here we see the great difference between them. ..ew exactly what would make the most telling effect upon a great number of people, and he never spent his strength on details which people could not appreciate. Bach lavished all his immense power upon producing the most perfect piece of art whether his hearers could understand it all or not.

### BACH'S LATIN CHURCH MUSIC

We must not leave the subject of Bach's vocal music without a word upon quite a different aspect of it, his setting of Latin words, in particular the *Magnificat* and the Mass. The *Magnificat* was written to be sung at Christmas time in St. Thomas's Church at Leipzig, and except for the fact that the Latin words are used, it is practically a church cantata of the German kind. At the first performance chorales were sung between its several movements, and one such tune is actually introduced into the work itself, played by the oboe, while a trio of voices sing 'Suscepit Israel puerum suum, recordatus misericordiae suae' ('He remembering his mercy hath holpen his servant Israel'). Most of the words are set to solo arias, with great choral numbers at the beginning and end. In the middle the chorus is used twice, and each time for a special, realistic purpose. It breaks in with the words 'Omnes generationes' ('all generations') to give the effect of a multitudinous consent, and again, 'Fecit potentiam in brachio suo, dispersit superbos mente cordis sui' ('He hath showed strength with his arm, He hath scattered the proud in the imagination of their hearts'), is set in a most graphic way. The voices are literally scattered at the word 'dispersit'; 'superbos' is shouted disdainfully by all the voices on a powerful discord, and a solemn ending seems to meditate on 'the imagination of their hearts'.

Bach wrote several masses, and parts of them were sometimes performed in the Lutheran churches of Leipzig, but his great Mass in B minor is written on a scale which makes it altogether beyond the bounds of any church service, Catholic or Protestant. It was written at various times, and probably represented to the composer's mind an ideal of musical worship which he never expected to be fully realized in any church. Now it is only to be heard in concert performance.

As in the *Magnificat*, so in the Mass there are places where Bach deliberately illustrates the meaning of special words by some feature of his music. Such are the wonderful passages in the Credo, where the voices all sink down to low, soft tones on the words, 'Passus et sepultus est' ('He suffered and was buried'), and after a moment's pause break out again with an exhilarating ascending phrase—'et resurrexit' ('and rose again'), and the even more wonderful one near the end of the Credo which introduces the words 'et expecto resurrectionem mortuorum' ('and I look for the resurrection of the dead') by a series of chords passing boldly out of the key of D major to harmonies which are not clearly related to any single key-note, and which seem to give a glimpse of limitless eternity. But the chief splendour of the Mass does not consist in these flashes of imaginative insight, beautiful though they are, but in the power with which the interest is maintained through the long succession of great choruses, solos, and duets, amongst which the words of the liturgy are divided. In order to do so, Bach draws upon every known style of music in turn. The ancient church plainsong is introduced into two passages of the Credo, the opening and the 'Confiteor unum baptisma' ('I believe in one baptism'), and in these and other choruses, especially the 'Gratias agimus' ('we give thanks'), the older polyphonic style of Palestrina is used to a large extent. Again, in one instance—the 'Crucifixus'—an overwhelming effect of brooding sorrow is produced by the use of a ground bass continually descending in semitones (cf. Purcell, p. 82). The arias, on the other hand, are full of the influence of Italian composers in their definite ternary form and the frequent use of florid ornamental passages (see especially

'Laudamus te'), but the deep feeling underlying the form is all Bach's own, whether it be the gladness of the soprano aria just named or the intensely earnest prayer of the contralto, 'Agnus Dei'. All the florid passages are there to express something, not to show off the singer's voice, and in no case is the singer allowed to be the chief object of interest, since an equal share of the music falls to some special instrument, violin, oboe, or horn, which is of as much importance as the voice.

Many of the choruses are examples of Bach's extraordinarily varied use of fugal writing; and as it would be impossible to explain the elements of this in connexion with such huge examples of its use, we will not attempt to study them. We will consider fugue later in connexion with Bach's and Handel's purely instrumental works, which illustrate its characteristics more simply.

Before leaving the subject we must see how far the growth of music has reached since the Masses of Palestrina appeared. Not only has the use of instruments produced quite new forms and means of expression such as the ground bass and the Italian aria, but whereas the first instrumental writers often made their instruments move with the smoothness of voices, Bach makes his voices move with all the force of instruments. The 'Kyrie Eleison' No. 1 ('O Lord have mercy'), one of the greatest fugues ever written, shows this at once, for instruments and voices play and sing the subject alike, yet its strong rhythm and its difficult intervals evidently come from a mind which knows that all intervals and rhythms can be played with equal certainty by the instruments, and what they do the voices must do. The definite rhythms and use of harmonies which, though sometimes dissonant in themselves, are quite understandable, because they all are founded upon a key system, show the technical advance of Bach and of Handel beyond the limits of the old church composers, and we have seen that these things put an immense increase of expressive power at their disposal. Without a clear system of key such a passage as Bach's 'Et expecto' (see above) would be powerless, for it would have no starting-point, and without a measured rhythm so vivid an outburst as Handel's 'Hallelujah' chorus in *Messiah* had been equally impossible.

Palestrina's most beautiful visions were always rather vague, Handel's were strong and somewhat material. Bach linked the mystic beauty of the one with the strength of the other.

## *Suggestions for Further Reading and Listening*

FROM now on further reading will be concerned entirely with the music of Bach and Handel, and what is here suggested will as a matter of course cover the final chapter of this volume as well as the present one, since few books separate the vocal from the instrumental music of the two masters, as the present one happens to do. The same is not true of gramophone records, needless to say, so that only those of a number of vocal works will be suggested here, while instrumental music will be noted in its proper place.

The handiest and cheapest guide-books are those in the 'Musical Pilgrim' series, small paper-covered pamphlets dealing with various single masterpieces or series of masterpieces by great composers. Two deal with Bach's vocal music, both by C. Sanford Terry, one being on the B minor Mass, the other on the Cantatas and Oratorios. Handel is not represented in this series, but *Handel: a Symposium*, edited by Gerald Abraham, contains admirable studies of various categories of his work by first-rate authorities. There is a detailed pamphlet on *Messiah* by E. C. Bairstow, and Julian Herbage's volume on the same work in the 'World of Music' series is worth reading, and is particularly interesting for its many illustrations. For various aspects of Handel's work the books by Dent and Young must be recalled (see p. 104); for Bach's those of Spitta and Schweitzer. W. Gillies Whittaker's *Fugitive Notes* deals far more solidly with some cantatas and the motets of Bach than the title suggests. Dr. Young's *The Oratorios of Handel* is well worth study; a larger work on the same subject, by Winton Dean, is in preparation (1956).

Gramophone resources now become very rich, so that any one consulting the record catalogues for specimens of Handel and Bach will be able to make a list embarrassing by wealth rather than by paucity. Suitable examples will no doubt be found as opportunity offers, but a few random notes may here be made. If a comparison of a Scarlatti *da capo* aria with one from a Handel opera has not already been made in connexion with Chapter IV, you should make one now; but unless the incident from *Giulio Cesare* referred to can be played on the piano—and it is worth bearing in mind that piano illustrations by small extracts always remain useful—an aria from that opera sung in German had better be avoided, particularly that which has on its reverse side an alleged 'cantata' entitled *Dank sei dir, Herr*, which is not Handel at all, but a pure fabrication. Handel's operatic arias should be sung in Italian, though in England an English translation may pass, as a German one may in Germany, provided there is no pretence that it is the original.[1] For everything else English is, of course, the proper language.

The Bach cantatas are comparatively neglected by the gramophone; still, it is easy enough to choose a representative extract, and very desirable that this should be done. On the other hand, the B minor Mass and the *St. Matthew Passion* are recorded complete or (the latter) nearly so, and the difficulty here will be to know what to omit rather than what to use. The choice, however, is best left to each person's taste. This is true, too, of specimens of Bach and Handel chosen for a comparison of the two masters' style and emotional response, and it is obvious that their setting of words of roughly the same content will show both similarities and differences most clearly.

[1] There is still a tendency in Germany to represent Handel as a German composer through and through, although there is nothing Germanic about his style, to be vague about his biography after his settling in London, and silent about the fact that, with very few exceptions, the words of his vocal works are Italian and English.

# CHAPTER VI

# *Instrumental Music of Handel and Bach*

WHILE it is quite possible to compare and contrast the music which Handel and Bach wrote for voices, a similar comparison is out of the question with regard to their music for instruments alone. Handel never devoted his attention to music of this kind in a wholehearted way. It is true that he wrote works of almost every kind then existing for various instruments, but they were always rather the offshoots of his genius written either for some special occasion, to fill up a blank space in his concert programmes, or for the benefit of his fashionable pupils. Bach, on the other hand, began life as an instrumental composer, and much of his earlier time was devoted to composition for his own instrument—the organ. Then, as we have seen, when he was at the height of his powers during the time that he spent at Köthen (1717–23) he gave himself up to the composition of music for instruments alone, and produced a great mass of splendid works of every conceivable kind, and in doing so he formed a style of his own which was quite unlike that of any of his predecessors or contemporaries. Consequently his work for instruments marches far ahead of Handel's, and to try to compare the two would be very unfair to Handel, for viewed in the light of Bach's music, his appears much less significant. Nevertheless there are beautiful things in Handel's works of almost every kind, and if we consider that most of them were very rapidly written, thrown off as it were in the spare moments of his busy life, we can realize something of the strength of his genius from them.

## HANDEL'S INSTRUMENTAL MUSIC

Handel's instrumental music can be divided for our purpose into three classes, and we shall look only at a few examples in each class. There is (1) music for the harpsichord alone which was equivalent to piano music, and is now often played on the piano; (2) chamber music, that is to say sonatas for two or three instruments intended to be played in private houses rather than in public, of which those for harpsichord and violin are now the best known; (3) music for an orchestra. This last includes a number of concertos for the organ accompanied by the orchestra which Handel used to play between the parts of his oratorios, as well as some concertos for orchestral instruments, and further, the overtures and other pieces which were included in his operas and oratorios.

### HARPSICHORD MUSIC

The harpsichord music consists of suites, lessons, fugues, and other pieces, many of which were written for pupils. We have already mentioned the suites and lessons of Purcell and the *ordres* of Couperin, and Handel's were planned in much the same way except that he did not confine himself to dance-tunes at all to the same extent as they, and instead of having a great number of little pieces in one suite he generally preferred to have only four or five, and to make them longer than the older writers were able to do. The actual order of pieces in a suite was always a matter for the composer's own taste, but still there were certain arrangements which were the most usual; for instance the suite generally began with a movement called either Prelude (which means something that is played first) or an Allemande, that is a German piece in a quick and fluent style. A Courante, an old French 'running' dance, would generally follow, and after it a Sarabande would frequently come, since it was a slow dance which contrasted well with the quick ones that had gone before. Next would come one or more Minuets, a Gavotte, and possibly others, with a quick dance, preferably the Gigue, to make a cheerful ending. Handel's suites contain movements of all these kinds, but they do not appear at all in the accepted order. Several of them have both a prelude and an allemande, as the first has. The second begins with an adagio, the fourth with a fine fugue which, properly speaking, has no place in the suite form. Some of them contain airs with variations, such as the fifth suite, which ends with the tune known, for reasons quite unconnected with the composer, as 'The Harmonious Blacksmith'.

The main point to realize, however, is that Handel's suites are not planned on any fixed form; he wrote any set of movements which would group well together, and generally the best movements were not the allemandes, courantes, and sarabandes which were the common property of suite writers, but those which he imported, as it were, from other kinds of work, such as the fugues (Suites IV and VIII[1]), the presto which ends Suite III, in which two themes are contrasted in a highly original way. The gigues, however, are an exception, for Handel had a special fondness for their delightful rhythm which, like Scarlatti, he had probably caught from Corelli when he was a young man in Italy (see p. 58). Sometimes when he has started a really good gigue theme it seems as though his delight in it would never stop, and as though he were determined to show that the dancers would be exhausted long before his powers of invention would be. The gigue ending Suite IX in G minor is a splendid example.

There is another interesting peculiarity in several of Handel's suites. Instead of letting all the movements stand apart from one another as quite separate things having no musical connexion, he would use the same theme as the groundwork of more than one movement. This was quite opposed to the old idea of a suite, which was that the movements should be as unlike as possible. Compare the openings of

> Suite IV.  Allemande and Courante.
> Suite VII. Andante and Allegro.
> Suite IX. Allemande and Courante.
> Suite XI. Allemande and Courante.

You see at once that the first few notes which form the theme

---

[1] The numbers shown here are those of the Peters edition.

are much alike in the outline of the melody in each pair, though the rhythm is altered, and this is remarkable, because the method of altering the character of a tune by changing its rhythm is one of which more recent composers such as Liszt and Berlioz became very fond.

The moment when we have Handel's suites before us is a good one in which to find out a little more clearly what a **Fugue** is.

To do so we must go back to the distinction which we discovered in the first chapter between polyphonic and homophonic music (see pp. 4–5). Now the dances of the suites all belong more or less to the second class, that is to say, they are harmonized tunes. But a fugue is like a 'catch'; there must be several voices or parts of which sings or plays a tune which agrees in harmony with the others. Let us suppose for the sake of clearness that the fugue is sung by four people: treble, alto, tenor, and bass. The idea is that each should begin by singing the same fragment of melody, a fragment which is to be the chief point of the whole of the fugue, as the text is the chief point of a sermon. Suppose that the treble sings it first, the alto will have to sing it on lower notes because his voice is lower, and probably it will be transposed into the key of the dominant for him, four notes down. While the alto sings the subject the treble goes on singing a new tune called the counter-subject, which harmonizes with the subject, but is quite distinct from it. Next the tenor enters singing the subject an octave below the treble while the alto goes on to the counter-subject, and finally the bass voice begins an octave lower than the alto. So far the fugue is very much like a catch, for all the voices sing the same music in turn, only they do not sing it upon the same notes. But they do not follow each other singing the same music through the whole work as the singers of a catch do, for after each has sung the subject and the counter-subject there is no strict rule as to what shall happen next. The voices return from time to time to the subject and counter-subject, singing them now in one part, now in another, sometimes changing to another key or from the major to the minor, sometimes altering them or singing them in longer or shorter notes, and then as the fugue draws near to the end one voice may begin the subject and another enter also singing it before the first has finished, so that they seem to catch each other up. (This device is called a *stretto*.) The whole must be planned so as to give all the prominence possible to the subject itself, and so it is exceedingly important that the subject should be a really fine bit of music which it is worth while to make prominent.

The treatment of a subject in fugue is perfectly natural when it is sung by different voices or played upon different instruments, each one of which carries on its own part, and as we have seen, all the earlier polyphonic music was written for a number of different voices and written in that way in order that each might bear an equal part in the interest of the performance. But when the fugue is played on a single instrument, such as the harpsichord or the piano or the organ, it requires a certain amount of make-believe on the part of the listener. You have to imagine that there are several voices or instruments carrying on the separate parts, and to follow their course with your ears in order to understand what is going on.

You can see quite easily how the fugue got transferred from the real human voices to the pretended ones of the harpsichord if you compare No. 5 of the Six Grand Fugues by Handel (Peters ed., Book III) with the chorus 'They loathed to drink of the river' in his *Israel in Egypt*. Both have the same subject, and in spite of a good deal of difference in detail the two are practically the same piece of music. In the oratorio the bold subject with its hard-sounding sevenths seems to picture the disgust of the people at the polluted river; in the harpsichord fugue it is just as striking in effect even though it is not connected with any particular story. Your ear is caught every time that great striding subject comes in, and you listen for its contrast with the theme in descending semitones which grows up out of the counter-subject as the fugue advances. Notice especially bars 31–33 where the bass starts the subject and the

treble comes in with the same tune two octaves higher before
the bass has finished it. This gives a perfect example of the way
in which a subject stamps its character upon the whole course
of a fugue. The one in G in Suite IV, with its repeated B's like
three determined strokes of a hammer, and the one in F minor
from Suite VIII, the subject of which marches up the scale with
a dignified tread, are other capital examples. We shall consider
this aspect of the fugue more fully when we come to those of
Bach.

CHAMBER MUSIC

The most important things in Handel's chamber music are the
sonatas for one or two instruments with harpsichord *continuo*,
and those for a single flute, oboe, or violin are the only ones
which we shall study here.

For the most part they follow the plan of Corelli's works of
the same kind, having four movements, a slow one and a quick
one alternately, and the last one is generally written in the
characteristic rhythm (12-8 time) of the gigue. In writing them
Handel followed the custom which all his predecessors had
used, when the harpsichord was employed as an accompaniment
either to another instrument or to the voice. Instead of writing
everything that the harpsichord was to play he simply wrote
the bass and put certain figures under it to show what chords
the right hand was to supply. The Italian word *continuo* for
such a part indicates that this bass continued uninterruptedly
throughout and so did the upper parts improvised by the
player, except in rare cases where a passage was marked *tasto
solo*. The musical 'filling' thus depended on the taste of the
player, but in modern editions of such music it has been filled in
by a later musician in a style as much like that of the composer as
possible. You see then that sonatas of this kind were thoroughly
homophonic and not polyphonic, that is to say, the tune of the
violin was the chief thing, the bass was only important because
it made the harmony clear, and the middle parts were so much
less important that it was thought unnecessary to write them

down. This is not to say, however, that a *continuo* part was necessarily uninteresting; indeed, harpsichord players in the eighteenth century were specially trained in the art of playing from figured basses, and the best of them were capable of astonishing feats which often included fugal and other polyphonic passages. They also had to be well grounded in the art of ornamentation and were required to know the conventions governing the use of trills, especially at cadential points. The only written guidance, apart from the bass line, was the general outline of the harmony: the figures showed the basic chords to be used, and to these the player had to adhere.

Although Handel's style is generally larger and broader than Corelli's, one sometimes finds themes in these sonatas which remind one very much of Corelli. The beginning of the allegro in the Sonata in G minor (Peters ed., No. 3) is a case in point:

Ex. 28

You see the likeness at once if you compare this with the Allemande of Corelli's Sonata in E minor (Ex. 20, p. 58), and one can also see that in this instance Corelli's skill as a violinist led him to carry on the leaping intervals of the theme far more strongly than Handel did.

To see Handel at his best in these sonatas look at the first allegro of the one in A (Peters No. 1). It shows how firmly Handel had grasped the principles of contrasting one theme with another and one key with another, and by means of these twin contrasts he is able to carry on his music and to make it grow in intensity till it reaches a splendid climax at the close. The principal theme is a double one given out by the violin and the bass of the harpsichord (Ex. 29).

Handel in his finest moments could not bear to confine himself to a wholly homophonic style, and here, although the upper part of the harpsichord is mere added harmony, the bass and the

Ex. 29

violin continue to treat these two ideas in a free contrapuntal style almost like a fugue. After eight bars the two are reversed, the harpsichord playing the bold downward theme (*a*) and the violin replying with the more delicate upward figure of quavers (*b*). A little later on they come in again in the key of E (that is, the dominant), and then for a time they are left in order to develop a new theme which leads through various keys back to the return of the double theme in its original key of A. Here the violinist must play both parts of it at once on two strings in order that the harpsichord may enrich the interest with a new bass, and afterwards, if you trace it out, you will find that the harpsichord part is almost entirely made up of one or other of the themes (*a*) or (*b*), while the violin adds all sorts of decorative passages until it at last bursts in with (*a*), emphasizing its two prominent notes by strong chords, the harpsichord accompanying it with a rolling passage in quavers, and so the movement ends majestically.

### ORCHESTRAL MUSIC

We saw how the elder Scarlatti and others gradually sorted out, as it were, the mixed collection of instruments which the first experimenters, Monteverdi and others, had used, and how they decided upon the stringed instruments, violins, violas, violoncellos, and double basses, as the best foundation for an orchestra. It became recognized that every orchestra must contain a certain number of these, but a great deal of diversity continued to exist as to the use of wind instruments. Handel relied upon oboes and bassoons as a permanent part of his orchestra, and in many of his overtures to operas he got striking effects by contrasting their thick reedy tone with the sharper and clearer tone of the violins, as here:

Ex. 30

The oboe concertos seem to have had this object in view, for the oboes are not sufficiently prominent in them to take the place as solo instruments which the organ holds in the organ concertos, but they add a good deal of variety to the tone.

Most of the other wind instruments which belong to the modern orchestra were perfectly well known in Handel's day, but what was not so well known was how to combine them with the strings. He frequently used trumpets and drums when he wanted big effects, for instance, in some choruses of *Messiah*, such as 'For unto us' and 'Hallelujah', and in the first chorus of *Saul*, and in the last case there are parts for all the instruments we have named and three trombones as well. The same work, which is particularly rich in orchestration, has flutes in the funeral march, and the harp in the scene of David's playing before Saul and in the song 'Fly, fly, malicious spirit'. Four horns make their appearance in the opening chorus of the opera *Julius Caesar*, and later on in that opera the harp, lute, and *viola da gamba* are introduced in order to give a luscious colouring to the scene of Cleopatra's court. It would be easy to go on piling up instances of Handel's use of instruments for special effects, but the only point of mentioning a few is to show that all the instruments of Beethoven's orchestra were familiar to Handel with one important exception—the clarinet. Nevertheless, his normal orchestra was much smaller; we may say that it consisted of strings, oboes and bassoons, trumpets and drums (used sparingly), and that flutes, horns, trombones, and harp were all extra instruments.

This gives some notion of the means which Handel had at his disposal. The next thing is to see how he used them. His works for the orchestra alone consist chiefly of concertos with a few additions such as the 'Water Music' (p. 100) and 'Fireworks Music'. There are several sets of concertos, those already mentioned in which oboes (and occasionally flutes) take part, and twelve 'Grand Concertos' for stringed instruments only, in addition to the organ concertos. These last are the only ones in which there is a single solo instrument, and since Handel was accustomed to play the organ part himself he never took the trouble to write them out quite fully, but used to trust largely to his memory or to his inventive power at the moment to make them effective. The other concertos, called *Concerti grossi*, all bear much the same relation to Corelli's works of the kind as his violin sonatas do to that master's: that is to say, their general plan is like his, but they are freer and finer both in their musical ideas and in their treatment of those ideas. Handel adopted the same plan of having a group of solo players and a stringed band as an accompaniment (see p. 57); the group of soloists in the oboe concertos were the oboe players and a violinist; in the 'grand concertos' they were two violinists and a violoncellist. We need not examine them in detail, since almost any page from among them shows how well Handel knew what kind of passages are most effective on stringed instruments, and what varieties of sound can be obtained from them by grouping them in different ways. But with the wind instruments his skill was far less complete; he had not found out what kinds of passages were especially suited to the oboes and bassoons, for example, and consequently we often find them playing exactly the same kind of passage as the strings, the oboes either in unison with the violins or playing alternately with them.

In speaking of the orchestra you may often hear musicians talk of 'colour': the tone of each instrument is compared to the colours on a painter's palette. The art of combining them is indeed very similar to that of the painter, for when the tones of the instruments are well blended they produce an almost infinite number of subtle lights and shades which you would never have suspected could be got from the few simple tones of the separate instruments. Now, to use this common simile, in most of his work Handel only reached the power of laying on colours in a few broad washes, as the early Italian painters of frescoes in tempera did; but in a few instances he achieved the intimate combinations of sound which correspond to the more delicate effects of colour later painters used in their oil paintings.

This is a point which no amount of explanation or even the

study of scores can make really clear. You would perceive it most quickly by listening to an overture by Handel and a symphony by Beethoven at the same concert, but we will illustrate the point by two short quotations here, and expand it further when we are studying the later developments of the orchestra.

The opening of the first Chandos Anthem already shown as Ex. 30 (p. 133) demonstrates Handel's customary way of contrasting oboe tone and violin tone. The music for each is just the same and the variety depends simply on the fact that the two are of different qualities; they contrast as simply as blue and red in a picture.

Ex. 31

On the other hand, the passage from *Saul* quoted in Ex. 31 combines the instruments much more closely, and is rather exceptional in Handel's work for that reason. Of course, the massing of the heavier instruments (bassoons, trumpets, trombones, drum, and strings) on the rhythmic figure (♩. ♪ ♩) is an obvious effect; anyone would have thought of that, but notice the way in which the oboes and the violins are dovetailed into one another in the first bar, how in the third bar where the two violins have an imitative passage the colour of the oboe is added to the second violin to give it distinction, and finally how in the last bar but one the trombones enrich the harmony of the strings by adding parts in the middle of them.

Ex. 31 *(continued)*

Apart from its point as an illustration of Handel's method, it makes a capital first lesson in the art of reading a full score.

### BACH'S INSTRUMENTAL MUSIC

At this stage of our study it is tremendously important to realize the differences between the effects of the various instruments and to see that these different effects are brought about by the different ways in which the instruments are made. We have just been looking at some of them in Handel's work; now before taking up any of Bach's music we must look for a moment at the mechanism of the organ, the instrument on which he

Ex. 31 (*continued*)

played and for which he wrote so constantly in his younger years that all his life through his thoughts seemed to spring from the sounds of the organ, just as later Schumann's sprang from the piano and Wagner's from the orchestra.

In the first place the organ is by far the most complicated musical instrument that has ever been invented for one person to play upon. That, no doubt, is why people have called it 'the king of instruments', because it brings such a great number of sounds under the control of one player. This is how it does so. Suppose that the keyboard of the organ contains fifty-six notes (i.e. about four and a half octaves), then fifty-six pipes will be required in order to make each one of these notes 'speak'.

Ex. 31 (*concluded*)

When the player presses down the key, wind from the bellows passes into the pipe belonging to that key, and as long as the key is held down the escape of wind through the pipe continues, causing the vibrations which produce the note. So an organ note (unlike that of the harpsichord, in which the string is plucked, or the piano, in which it is struck by a hammer) can be sustained as long as the player chooses to hold the key.

An organ, however, with merely one pipe to each note of the keyboard, would be a very simple affair. As a matter of fact, every organ has a variety of sets of pipes called stops, which can be made to sound either together or separately on the same keyboard. In the case we are supposing, each of these sets would contain fifty-six pipes, a pipe to a key, and the great beauty in a fine organ is that each set of pipes (i.e. each stop) has a distinct quality of tone which all its pipes possess equally and which distinguishes it from the other stops. Some stops are loud, some soft; some, called diapasons, have a strong, rich tone which make them the groundwork of the organ as the stringed instruments are of the orchestra; others produce light and sweet sounds like flutes; others copy the sounds of orchestral instruments closely, such as oboes and trumpets, and all these may be made to sound the same note together when the player's finger presses the key, or any selection of them may be used. The great difference between the stops of the organ and the instruments of the orchestra is that the stops on one keyboard all sound the same notes when they sound at all. You cannot, for example, hold down a chord of C in which the oboe sounds the top C, the trumpet G, and the diapasons E and the lower C. If you had drawn those stops they would all sound the four notes. In order to get over this disadvantage to some extent the plan of building organs with two or three keyboards was invented, each keyboard having certain stops of its own, so that the organist could play with one hand on each, or pass quickly from one to another. By this means a diapason stop on one keyboard might be contrasted with, say, an oboe stop on another, and such an effect as Handel got in the Chandos Anthem (Ex. 30) could be reproduced almost exactly on the organ. Still this sort of contrast was, and still is, limited to what the player's two hands can contrive in passing from keyboard to keyboard, and it would be impossible to contrast the tones of the various stops with anything like the closeness of the orchestration in Ex. 31.

One more of the special resources of the organ must be borne in mind, namely, the pedals. The pedal-board is merely another keyboard, played by the feet instead of by the hands, but its notes only include about two and a half octaves, and so represent the bass part of the other keyboards. Its principal stops sound an octave below those of the hand keyboards (called manuals), just as the double-basses of the orchestra sound an octave below the violoncellos.

If you have been able to follow this description you will now see what the organ is capable of doing. First, it can produce as many different kinds of tone as there are stops, and it can combine them in many ways to produce fresh ones, just as a painter can mix blue and yellow and get green; but these combinations are limited by the fact that all the stops on one manual must play the same music. Secondly, in Bach's day the organist could only make his music louder or softer by using more or fewer stops, since each pipe always gives a constant amount of tone.[1] That means that no single stop was capable of any expression at all, since the only thing under the control of the player was the length that each note should last; he could not alter its loudness or its softness, or give any accent to one note over another. The organist has none of the power of the violinist, whose bow can both sustain a note perfectly and can at any moment produce an accent by a little more pressure. But then, on the other hand, a violinist can only play comparatively few chords, and can scarcely play polyphonic music at all, so that in such things the organist has a great advantage. His power of sustaining notes, and of playing with feet as well as hands, made him better at

[1] Nowadays this defect is partly remedied by the use of a 'swell'.

playing such music as fugues than even the harpsichordist, whose notes diminished rapidly in sound as soon as they were struck.

We are now ready to illustrate the capacities of the instrument by means of some of the music which Bach wrote for it. It has been said already that the amount of his music in every form is very great, and so it would be quite impossible to give even the shortest summary of what he wrote. Instead, we shall try to get some clear knowledge of two or three works which will give a notion of his style.

First, take the Toccata and Fugue in D minor, which is one of the most wonderful things he wrote to play on his organ at Arnstadt. The Toccata is short, but it contains almost every kind of effect obtainable on the organ. Its very first note, that A

with a little ornament of two notes upon it (played ),

shows how well Bach knew his instrument. If he had been writing for strings there would have been no need for that little turn; the bite of the bow would have given the necessary accent (cf. Beethoven's second Symphony or Leonora Overture No. III).

See what a force is added to the rapid descending phrases by the rests and pauses between them. These impressive silences make up for the lack of any accent on the organ, for they seize the attention as a good speaker does when he pauses before saying something of special importance. Then notice that massive discord (technically a dominant minor ninth on a tonic pedal) which is gradually spread out using all the big overwhelming sound of the instrument, and which finishes the phrase by sinking down into the quiet major chord. After this come long passages rolling up and down the compass of the instrument and again cut off by the same striking chord in a still fuller form. Notice also the repetitions and variations on this simple harmonic figure:

Ex. 32

*Ped.*

which of course can be enforced by the use of different stops, and the brilliant running passages which lead up to the last powerful phrase for the pedals, accompanied by detached chords played by the hands. This toccata has no definite melodic idea, it makes no attempt to develop a subject by any of the ordinary processes, but it compresses into a small space almost all the noble effects of sound which the organ can produce.

The fugue, too, is very unlike the examples by Handel which we studied. There is extraordinarily little counterpoint or interplay of parts in it, and many of its passages are not polyphonic at all, but consist of rushing scales and arpeggios, which are very effective on the organ, and require none of the thinking power on the part of the listener which most fugues call for. The flowing subject constantly recurs but is never used in *stretto* (see p. 129), and at the end Bach breaks away from the fugue style altogether and finishes by recalling some of the features of the toccata in a magnificent coda.

It is quite impossible to understand how in face of such pieces as this (and there are plenty more of the same kind) people could ever imagine that Bach was merely a learned man who wrote things hard to enjoy; but they did in his lifetime, and there are even some unfortunates who think so now.

It is natural that as he grew older and thought more deeply his music should take a more serious turn, and that he should grow to care more and more for the greater kinds of expression, which come from the development of fine ideas of melody, rhythm, and harmony, and care less for mere brilliant combinations of sound. So in his other Toccatas, the larger one in D minor and still more in the huge Toccata in F major, there are far fewer surprises for the listener, but the music is much more splendid and rich in design. It would take too long to analyse the Toccata in F in detail as we have the shorter one in D minor; everyone should hear it and compare it with the other for himself.

You will realize how tremendous is the sweep of the first theme, played in canon by the two hands while one long impressive note is sustained on the pedals; next, how the pedals at last burst out with a new version of the theme, and how closely the rhythm of the theme is adhered to until a fresh idea, a series of chords in detached pairs, makes its appearance, to be afterwards combined with the rolling semiquavers of the principal theme. The whole is on a gigantic scale, and while it is full of characteristic organ effects, they are not the things which seize and hold the attention. Rather they serve to set forward the majestic musical conception.

We shall not attempt to study Bach's wonderful power of fugal workmanship in his organ music. What makes his fugues greater than those of any other composer is the fact that he never allowed the artificial requirements of the form to interfere with the expression of his ideas, but used only those artifices which helped to make his ideas clearer and stronger. We shall be able to realize this more fully, however, when we look at the fugues in his clavier music (see p. 151).

There is, however, one other phase of music for the organ which is too important to be passed by, namely, the chorale preludes. We have already seen how dear the chorales were to the hearts of German Protestants, how Buxtehude and others made them the groundwork of their compositions, and how Bach himself built his cantatas upon them. His intense love of the chorales, and his power of bringing out all the nobility and tender sentiment of the old hymns by the music which he added

to the tunes, can be still better shown in the chorale preludes
written to be played on the organ. Some of these were meant
to be introductions to the hymns themselves when they were
sung in church, others, the longer and more elaborate ones, are
separate instrumental pieces, and some are actual arrangements
of movements from his cantatas.

The following are examples of various methods of treatment:

*Herzlich tut mich verlangen.* This is a setting of Hassler's lovely
tune (p. 85) which Bach used so often in his Passion music. The
way he treats it here is very remarkable, because the tune does
not appear at all in its simple form after the first bar. But if you
listen to it you will hear that though the tune is altered by the
little groups of semiquavers which take the place of plain
crotchets, its general outline is preserved, and those little ornaments as well as the rich harmonies impress the pathetic beauty
of the tune. Another more extended instance of the same way
of treating the tune is *O Mensch, bewein' dein' Sünde gross*, a
tune also used in the St. Matthew Passion. Contrast with these
the setting of the old Christmas carol, *In dulci jubilo*. Here two
parts, the treble and the bass, play the tune in canon, and while
they do so joyful triplet figures are added, like the pealing of
Christmas bells.

*Nun danket alle Gott* shows yet another method. The tune is
played in long notes in the treble and the other three parts lead
up to each phrase by passages in quicker notes in the manner of
a fugue, so that every time a bit of the melody appears in the
treble it seems to explain the more complicated music which
has just passed in the other parts.

One more example must be our last, and it is worthy to be,
for Bach never in his whole life wrote anything more beautiful.
It is *Wachet auf*, an arrangement of a movement in the Advent
cantata of that name (see p. 114). Again, the chorale is played
through in detached phrases, this time in a tenor part (it is the
tenors who sing it in the cantata). But there is no complex
fuguing to accompany it. Instead, the organist's right hand
is employed in playing another beautiful melody which has

nothing whatever to do with the chorale and does not seem to have any special descriptive purpose like the ringing bells of *In dulci jubilo*. It has, however, much to do with the words to which it belongs, for it overflows with the spirit of heart-felt joy expressed in

> Zion hört die Wächter singen,
> Das Herz tut ihr vor Freude springen.

There is one other point of view from which this melody must be studied. Its beauty depends chiefly on two features: (1) the rise and fall in pitch of its notes (e.g. the drop of a sixth in the first bar), and (2) the rate at which the notes move (i.e. the contrast of quavers with semiquavers), and the syncopations. Both pitch and rhythm are so perfect that the additions of accents on prominent notes or variations of loudness and softness are scarcely necessary to it. It is, therefore, like so many of Bach's best, a typical organ melody, in spite of the fact that he first wrote it for stringed instruments to play.

### CLAVIER MUSIC

With the clavier music—that is to say, music for either the harpsichord or the clavichord—we come to matter which is a good deal easier to understand than some of the questions which the organ music raises. This is because both the instruments called by the name of 'clavier' are much simpler in construction, and therefore produce simpler effects of sound than the organ, and, moreover, their music is so easily transferred to the piano, and sounds so well upon it, that we can appreciate it better than we can the less familiar organ music.

Again, however, we must remember what are the characteristics which distinguish the harpsichord from the clavichord, and both from the piano. When we first mentioned the harpsichord as used in Monteverdi's orchestra (p. 21) we spoke of the short, sharp tone got by plucking the string, and since the plucking was done by the mechanical action of a quill, the player could not control its loudness or softness any more than the organist could control the force of one of his organ stops. In other words, he could not play louder by hitting the keys harder as the pianist can, and he could not hold on a note by holding down the key as an organist can perfectly, and a pianist can to a certain extent. In order to get some varieties of tone, therefore, harpsichords were often made with two manuals like an organ, one loud and one soft, and in some instruments other alterations of the tone were contrived by means of stops, and sometimes pedals were added.

The clavichord, on the other hand, was quite a little instrument which could be carried about easily and stood on a table. Instead of being plucked, its strings were pushed by a little piece of metal called a 'tangent', and though it always produced a very soft sound, so soft that if any one spoke or moved while it was being played you could hardly hear it at all, yet the player could vary the degree of sound by the pressure of his fingers, and so in this most important respect it was more like the piano than any other keyed instrument of the time.

One can see why Bach loved the clavichord. He did not want to play to large numbers of people who fidgetted and made noises as people in drawing-rooms and concert-rooms always do; he played for the love of music and for the pleasure of the few who would sit near him and listen. So he delighted in the gentle little clavichord, the only keyed instrument which could produce the delicate lights and shades of expression.

The pieces included in the two books which together make up the 'Forty-eight Preludes and Fugues' were written at a great many different times and collected together by Bach in two series. The first twenty-four were put together while he was at Köthen, that is, in the time when his energies were particularly concentrated upon instrumental music, and he only finished the second set of twenty-four quite late in life at Leipzig. They are therefore spread out over many years, and if we knew when each was written they would make a sort of musical diary of Bach's thoughts and feelings in the different circumstances of his existence, for they are so full of varied expression that there can be no doubt that they represent very strong personal feeling.

The order in which the pieces are placed depends neither upon the time when they were written nor on artistic considerations of contrast, but on the keys to which they belong. Bach's name for the first collection was 'Das wohltemperirte Klavier' ('The Well-tempered Clavier'), and each pair of pieces, prelude and fugue, is in a different key, major or minor, beginning from C major, followed by C minor, and so on in ascending semitones. The meaning of the rather curious term 'well-tempered' is a simple one. It alludes to the fact that an old-fashioned system of tuning instruments had survived from the time when very little change of key was used, and this system made the instruments beautifully in tune in certain keys, the more usual ones, and quite unbearable in others. A key would be tuned, for instance, to B♭ or F♯ in just intonation, but they would not serve for A♯ and G♭, as they do by the compromise of the tempered scale. Bach realized that such a plan barred the progress of instrumental music, for, as we have seen, much of its progress consisted in the gradual establishment of the key system, and the power which it brought to composers of passing from one key to another. Bach insisted in this work that all keys must be equally available for use, and that the instruments must be tuned or tempered in such a way as to make them so. Bach, then, asserts the freedom of the musician on the very title-page, and in his music he maintained the same attitude fearlessly. The form of each prelude depends solely upon the kind of ideas which have to be expressed; there is no fixed shape to which all conform, as there is in the sonatas of Domenico Scarlatti for example. Sometimes it is possible to analyse them into a number of component parts, e.g. Book I, No. 7, E flat major, which has an impressive introduction followed by a long movement worked out in the organ style of counterpoint, or Book I, No. 10, E minor, which begins with a sustained melody in the right hand, accompanied by a flowing semiquaver figure in the left, and which halfway through suddenly abandons the melody for the sake of developing the accompanying figure into a brilliant presto. Or again, most remarkable of all in point of form, there is the prelude in D major, Book II, No. 5, which is actually in the sonata form of a later age, that of Mozart and Haydn.

More constantly, however, the whole prelude is woven without a break. Bach's modulations are clear and strong, but when he passes to a new key he does not rest there, but his ever-moving melodies and rhythms force one's attention to go forward so that a total impression is left of something indivisible. The actual expression of the preludes is very rich and varied. In the first book, for example, No. 1, C major, is a dreaming succession of beautiful harmonies played with just enough rhythmic interest to give them vitality; No. 4, C sharp minor, springs out of a fragment of melody one bar long, very tender in feeling, which is treated polyphonically by the two hands and extended into a lovely song; No. 5, D major, is a 'moto perpetuo' for the right hand, its rhythm emphasized by the piquant staccato notes of the left hand; and No. 8, E flat minor, is a wonderful romance. Pay special attention to this one. Notice the persistent throbbing chords, three in the bar, and the beauty of the melody added above them. As the piece advances this melody becomes a duet in which both hands take part, and the feeling is made more intense by the use of some unexpected harmonies. Twelve bars before the end the piece seems to be about to close with a cadence, but it is interrupted with a powerful discord, and the melody is continued until four bars from the end a similar point is reached. Again, however, the close is avoided by a strong chord of the seventh, as though Bach could not bear to leave so lovely an idea. This way of expressing deep feeling by means of poignant harmonies was rare (cf. Purcell, pp. 82–83). It was undreamt-of by the older writers, and even Handel rarely tried it, but it is one which later writers, especially Chopin and Wagner, adopted with wonderful results (cf. Chopin's Prelude in E minor, No. 4, and Wagner's prelude to *Tristan*).

The relationship of the preludes to the fugues which follow them is remarkably interesting. In some cases it seems as though Bach wished to correct the impression made by the prelude, and so followed it with a fugue of different character; in other cases the fugue carries on the feeling of the prelude to a further point. As examples of the first look again at Nos. 1, 4, 5, and 8 of the first book; three of them, 1, 4, 8, have preludes which are rather sad and very full of sentiment. They all have fugues particularly strong and virile in style, packed full of devices which need keen thought for their appreciation. The prelude of No. 5, on the other hand, is light-hearted, and perhaps a bit frivolous; Bach gives it a fugue of very sturdy rhythm. This must not be taken to imply that the preludes were thought of first and the fugues after, but simply that he chose to mate these movements according to the law of contrast. The Prelude in E minor, No. 10, on the contrary seems actually to grow up to the fugue. We have already seen how its accompanying figure becomes the chief object of interest, and the fugue subject is only one more step in its development. No. 12 is another good instance of both prelude and fugue building upon the same kind of idea, in this case the effect of a pathetic tune in crotchets combined with semiquavers.

It would be a good exercise of the imaginative faculties to go through some of the fugues playing merely the subject of each in its right tempo and with proper phrasing, and trying to name its character by a single adjective; thus No. 1 is stately, No. 2 playful, No. 3 graceful, No. 4 thoughtful, and No. 5 we have already found to be sturdy. If we go a step farther and ask why they suggest these qualities we find that it is because of special features in their melody or rhythm. The measured rise and fall of No. 1 gives it its stateliness, the little pairs of semiquavers make No. 2 playful, the rise of the sixth after the turn gives grace to No. 3, and that peculiar interval of a diminished fourth, which is so hard to sing accurately, suggests thought in connexion with No. 4. You will find as you study the fugues that generally the character of the subject is thoroughly justified

in the working out of the fugue, and that the fresh music added
to the subject helps to emphasize the same qualities. The first
fugue is so full of its subject that there scarcely seems to be
anything else; there is hardly a moment where there is not one
part playing it, and towards the end they intertwine so closely
that from bar 14 onward all four are playing different parts of
the subject at one time. No. 2, on the contrary, is too cheerful for
any such serious process. There is no *stretto* at all; instead the
subject gets broken up into little fragments which are bandied
about between the parts, and added to them are some delicate
running semiquaver passages which play hide and seek with
the merry subject. Similarly, the grace of No. 3 might be spoilt
if Bach indulged in elaborate fugal work, so he avoids it, and
instead he presents the subject and the flowing counter-subject
in all sorts of new and graceful figures. But with No. 4 he becomes very serious again, for not content with the solemn
subject (*a*) with which he begins:

Ex. 33

he afterwards thinks of two more quite independent ones (*b*
and *c*), which join with it and appear in a number of relationships.

These are a few indications of the types of variety to be found
in the first numbers of the '48'; similar illustrations could be
drawn from any other group in either series, and their most
marvellous quality of all is the fact that, however well they are
known, one can always discover some fresh beauty in them.

The many works by Bach in the form of the suite show us a
very different side of his character. The principal ones are a set

of six small works called 'French' Suites, another larger set known as the 'English' Suites, and six more called 'Partitas'. The first were written in the book which Bach compiled for his second wife, and they probably got their name from the fact that the pieces are all very concise and are written in the simple forms which Couperin and other French clavecinists had used so well (see pp. 71–73).

Bach did not treat the suite form with the same freedom that Handel did. We saw that except the gigues, which are full of the feeling of the dance, Handel's best pieces were the preludes, fugues, and overtures which he included but which, properly speaking, have nothing to do with the suite as a form. Bach wrote no fugues in his suites, and their beauty for the most part rests upon the characters of the dance-tunes. It was in this respect that he learnt much from the example of Couperin, as can be seen by comparing his 'French' Suites with the pieces of Couperin. Bach did not give his dances descriptive titles as Couperin did, but one cannot hear his suites played without realizing how much trouble he took to make the various pieces of the same name contrast with one another. Compare for example the dignified Sarabande in D minor ('French' Suites, No. 1) with the fairy-like melody of the one in C minor (No. 2), or the plaintive one in G major (No. 5). Again he frequently wrote two minuets in the same suite and always made them contrast very strongly with each other, e.g. the pair in the Suite in B minor, the first of which is light and fluent, the second more wayward and continually changing its key. But the six gigues, one of which ends each suite, show the greatest variety of any. One point in which they are alike is the fact that they all have the rhythm of alternate long and short notes, but this very simple rule admits of countless variations of design. If you look at the Gigue in D minor (No. 1) and then at the one in G major (No. 5) you would scarcely suppose that they represent the same dance. The one in E (No. 6) is most like the straightforward style which Handel learnt from the Italians, and several numbers in the 'English' Suites are like them, but the first three in the 'French' Suites all try rather new experiments in rhythm, and several are so polyphonic as almost to have the effect of fugues. Indeed, Bach's way of combining polyphonic parts with the dance forms is one of the beauties of his suites. Couperin had done this in some instances, but it was a part of Bach's very nature, for he loved the deep tones got by the inter- weaving parts more than any other type of instrumental effect. Consequently, however much he learnt from the Italians—and he did learn a great deal, especially in writing his concertos—he always gave greater depth of feeling to his work because his mind moved in many directions at once. It was not enough for him to express his musical ideas in clear melodies of definite and balanced form with a substratum of harmony; every detail of harmony was important to him, and every part contributed both to the rhythm and colour of the whole work, whether it were a simple dance-tune or the most elaborate fugue.

CHAMBER MUSIC

Bach's concertos for one or more harpsichords with accom- paniment for strings and those for one or more violins might be included under the comprehensive term 'chamber music', for they were not intended for the big concert performances in which we now often hear them. But instead we will draw our examples from the six sonatas for violin and harpsichord, and the six for violin alone. His thorough treatment of details especially in the harpsichord part is perfectly seen in the beauti- ful slow movements which begin the Sonatas for violin and harpsichord in B minor and E major (Nos. 1 and 3), the two which are most often played. The chief feature of the one in B minor is a tender figure of quavers phrased in pairs. This begins in the right hand of the harpsichord part and is continued while the violin enters with a flowing melody above it. Later on the violin joins in the characteristic figure, playing it in chords. Such a movement would have been quite impossible in a com- position in which the details of the harpsichord part were left to the player to devise, as Handel and the Italians left them. It gains all its expressiveness from the way in which the two instruments treat the figure on equal terms. The Adagio of the Sonata in E has another device. Here the two do not develop the same music together, but each has a theme of its own and the two are contrasted. That of the harpsichord consists of a short group of notes constantly repeated and afterwards extended while the violin plays a long free melody full of ornamental and decorative passages. A few places will be found in these sonatas where harmonies are indicated by figures below the bass and not written out in full, but they are so exceptional as to show how little Bach dared to trust to such a casual plan.

The general form of the sonatas is exceedingly free. The movements owe nothing to the traditional dance forms. They bear no titles except Andante, Allegro, &c., which of course are merely indications of the pace at which they are to be played. An exception to this is the movement beginning the Sonata in C minor, called Siciliano, that is to say a dance popular in Sicily, which was like the gigue in rhythm but slower and smoother. The Italian writers used it often in their sonatas, and Bach's use of it, enriching it with beautiful arpeggio figures for the harpsichord, shows how he would adopt their methods and improve upon them.

Nothing is more extraordinary in the style of Bach's instrumental music than the way in which his devotion to organ music affected his work for the violin alone. These two instruments have nothing in common except the power of sustaining tone. The organist, as we saw, cannot make any of the subtle variations of quality which are the chief resource of the violinist; and the violinist has very little of that power of playing in polyphonic parts and producing big chord effects which the organist can command, yet in these sonatas Bach transferred as much as was possible of the organ style to the violin. He could not forgo his rich effects of many moving parts, and he found that even though the violin cannot maintain them, a skilful player can suggest them by rapidly passing from string to string, and by playing on two strings at once. The most celebrated of all his works of the kind is the great chaconne which ends the Sonata in D minor. When this is well played the amount of polyphonic effect is amazing, and the force of the big chords in which the theme is announced, contrasting with the brilliant variations which follow, make it the most wonderful piece ever written for a single violin without accompaniment. The fugues are further examples of Bach's skill in making the effects of organ music adaptable to the violin. Another movement which is often played apart from the sonata to which it belongs is the Gavotte en rondeau from the Sonata in E. This is a French form (cf. Lully's gavotte in *Armide*, p. 68), and of course has nothing to do with organ music, but again the rich harmony which gives almost the effect of a whole band of violins is of the kind which only Bach would have attempted to convey by means of one alone, and the same is true of many of the dance movements in these works.

## ORCHESTRAL MUSIC

It would seem that whenever Bach wrote for instruments with which daily use had not made him thoroughly familiar, he was apt to draw upon his experiences as an organist. In writing for the harpsichord or clavichord he was least inclined to do so, for he knew perfectly what they were capable of doing; we know that he played the violin, but he did not live with it as constantly as he did with the keyed instruments, and consequently the organ influence is strong in his solo music for it, and again it is very prominent in his music for the orchestra. This is not surprising since there is much in common between the organ and the orchestra, but the organ is so much more limited than the orchestra that the one is rather misleading as a preparation for the other. Bach had an even keener feeling for the varieties of tone-colour than Handel, and he used all the instruments which Handel used and tried many different ways of combining them. But he was constantly inclined to treat them like so many stops of the organ, and to write the same kind of passage for them all as though they were all played in the same way, and could all manage the same music equally well. It is a disadvantage which serves to show that even he who accomplished so much did not succeed in mastering quite all the problems of musical workmanship, but it does not cloud the glory of the music which he wrote for the orchestra. His chief works of the kind are the six 'Brandenburg' Concertos (so called because they were written for the Margrave of Brandenburg while Bach was at Köthen), and four overtures which are fine examples in the style of Lully's operatic overtures with groups of dances added.

It is most probable that Bach never heard the Brandenburg Concertos played since he presented them to the Margrave, who was one of those people who care more for collecting works of art than for using them when they have got them, and so they were put away in his library and forgotten.

The only feature of these concertos which is like those of the Italians is the fact that in three cases the instruments are divided into the groups of soloists and accompanists, called by the Italians the *concertino* and *ripieno* respectively, but even in this as well as in the choice of instruments for each group Bach allowed his fancy to have free play, and seems to have thought only of what arrangement would express his ideas best in each case. Thus the first is written for a rather large orchestra in which strings, three oboes, bassoon, and two horns take part all on more or less equal terms. The group of solo instruments in the second is very unusual; it consists of a trumpet, a flute, an oboe, and a violin, while a full band of strings form the *ripieno*. No. 3 is for strings only, divided into ten parts, i.e. three violins, three violas, three violoncellos, and a bass, and the contrasts gained between the groups are extraordinarily subtle and beautiful. No. 4 has as its solos a violin and two flutes; No. 5 a harpsichord, a violin, and a flute, both being accompanied by strings, and the last, like the third, consists of an uncommon arrangement of strings, since it is scored only for two violas, two viole da gamba (nowadays generally played as violoncello parts), violoncello, and bass.

The Brandenburg Concertos, as it happens, sound quite

complete without a supporting harpsichord *continuo*, and are usually so played nowadays. But the convention of the time was that all orchestral music of this type, and indeed much else, such as the arias in operas and oratorios for instance, should be supported by a keyboard instrument (in some cases the organ), whether a *continuo* part was provided by the composer or not, and whether he had figured his basses or not. Even where a solo keyboard instrument forms part of a work, as in the fifth Brandenburg Concerto, a supporting harpsichord was still used; and the habit was so strong that even where it was not actually wanted, as here, the *continuo* persisted. Orchestral works as late as Haydn's early symphonies still retained it.

Nos. 2, 3, 4, 5 are all frequently played at concerts, No. 6 more rarely, and No. 1 scarcely ever. Probably the elaborate writing for the horns accounts for the neglect of the first, for Bach seems to have considered that so long as he kept the parts within the possible compass of the instruments the horns should be able to play anything he chose to write for them, and so he requires them to run about with almost the agility of a flute. This concerto also differs from all the others in the fact that added to the usual three movements are some charming dances, a minuet, and *polacca* (i.e. a Polish dance), each with a trio scored for small groups of instruments; the trio to the minuet is for oboes and bassoons only, and that to the *polacca* is for horns and bassoons. They remind one of the kind of music of which Haydn and Mozart afterwards wrote so much as *divertimenti* and serenades.

Unlike the others which have three movements, a slow one between two quick ones, the third Concerto has only two, and both are full of joy and good spirits. The strong pulsing rhythm of the tunes and the way they are divided between the stringed instruments, which at one moment are spread out into ten parts, at another massed together into broad unison passages, gives the impression of bounding energy and happiness.

We will take the second Concerto as our chief example of Bach's orchestral music and look more closely at the score.

There is one point which must be explained at the outset, because it will be met with in all the later orchestral music of Haydn, Mozart, and Beethoven, so it had better be understood at once—i.e. the principle of writing for what are called the 'transposing' instruments of the orchestra. We get an example of it here in the trumpet part placed at the head of the score. The natural trumpets and horns for which Bach wrote are merely tubes without any keys such as oboes possess. All the different notes, therefore, have to be produced by the varying pressure of the player's lip, and the possible notes range over about two octaves, say, middle C to the C above the treble stave. But it is impossible to get all the notes lying between these extremes. In the lower octave only the notes of the common chord, and in the upper octave those of the diatonic scale, but not all the semitones between them, are available. Bach's trumpet part in the first pages of this Concerto shows clearly what notes the trumpet could play. But in order that the trumpets (and horns) might be used in different keys, pieces of tubing called 'crooks' were added so as to transpose this series of notes into the key of the work, in this instance F. In Bach's time, however, composers always wrote as though these instruments were playing in the key of C, since they had only to put on the proper crook at the beginning in order to make it sound in the right key. This was perhaps simpler for the players, but it is harder for us who have to read the score, since we have to remember that the trumpet is not playing the notes written, which of course would sound excruciating, but is really playing in F like the rest of the orchestra. So the first phrase of the trumpet part sounds as here:

Ex. 34

Having disposed of preliminaries we come to the music. All the instruments begin with a brilliant and lively tune of a rhythm which is unforgettable once it is heard. When this is completed the solo violin creeps in with a more gentle theme which becomes the principal one of the soloists, for they all play it in turn with constant interruptions from the string band who burst in with fragments of the first theme. The whole of the first movement consists of these tunes woven together in all sorts of relationships; sometimes the tunes of the four solo instruments are contrasted with one another, sometimes they are massed together to contrast with the strings; at one time the soloists are all rushing about in florid passages while the strings hold long chords, then the violins mutter the rhythm of their chief tune (*piano*) while the soloists play bits of it in a bold *stretto* (*forte*). The trumpet is left out of the tender little slow movement, and the three other soloists with the violoncellos to accompany them have it all to themselves. Here you can see how Bach treats his instruments as if they were organ stops, and indeed the violoncello part suggests the pedals very obviously. Flute, oboe, and violin all develop the lovely melody in the same way, sometimes combining in harmony, but more often in passages which imitate one another very beautifully. Especially notice the delicate effect of the simple phrases of three or four notes which in the latter part are passed from one to the other. The trumpet after being silent for so long leads off the last movement with a merry tune which the others take up and treat in a free fugal manner. The string accompaniment of this is all much lighter than in the first movement; there is little of the intricate weaving of parts, but for the most part the violins play short detached quavers which add sparkle and brightness to the solo music. The whole is full of the sense of fun and jollity carried on to the very last bars where the trumpet begins the tune afresh, the others harmonizing it as though it were going to modulate into the key of B♭, when the music stops abruptly and takes every one by surprise.

These surprises are perhaps the most fascinating things in Bach's music. He knew thoroughly all that other composers in Italy and France had done, and he often chose to work according to their methods, especially as regards the form of his music, but he never bound himself to follow the lead of any one. All through his music one finds these evidences of a fresh and unfettered spirit which are all the more delightful because he never introduced them unless he meant something by them.

Bach's nature was so many-sided that his music touches almost every phase of human feeling from the irresponsible gaiety of this movement or the comicality of *Phoebus and Pan* to the deep sorrow of the Passion music, or the majestic splendour of the Mass in B minor. That is why his music appeals to men of such widely different tastes and ways of thought, so that although musical people differ and even quarrel about the greatness or worth of almost every other composer the name of Bach unites them all.

## *Suggestions for Further Reading and Listening*

THE books by Spitta and Schweitzer on Bach, and by Dent and Young on Handel, already recommended for general reading, will have been found to cover a good deal that is discussed in the present chapter. The Handel symposium edited by Gerald Abraham will serve more specifically with such chapters as deal with that master's instrumental music. Two more 'Musical Pilgrim' booklets on Bach are to be had dealing with instrumental works, both by J. A. Fuller-Maitland: one on the Brandenburg Concertos, and the other on *The Well-Tempered Clavier*. On the last there is also Cecil Gray's *The Forty-Eight Preludes and Fugues of J. S. Bach. The Organ Works of Bach* by Harvey Grace concerns itself closely with that large subject in general. Sir Donald Tovey's *Companion to 'The Art of Fugue'* will be found indispensable by those who wish to take in a great work not discussed here in detail. *Bach's Ornaments* by Walter Emery contains much incidental information.

Records which may serve as examples of the music we have discussed will be so easily found that it would be almost an impertinence to make detailed suggestions. If the text of this chapter is followed, all sorts of useful specimens will come to mind at once, and record guides and catalogues will show material for more extended study, if that is desired. More useful than to prescribe what may be used, perhaps, is an indication of what to avoid. There is so much music by both Bach and Handel now recorded in the original that there is no excuse for resorting to any arrangements or transcriptions whatsoever in the case of Bach, while for Handel only the Harty versions of the 'Water' and 'Fireworks' Music should be allowed to pass, and those merely because no records in the original scoring, which was specially designed for the open air, and would doubtless sound raucous and uncouth, are to be had. Both the Harty suites have been arranged for the piano, and there is no harm in playing separate numbers or extracts in that form, since in any case it is a question of an arrangement or nothing. Whether for the keyboard works any records using the piano in place of the harpsichord or clavichord are to be admitted is more debatable: on the whole the authentic instruments are certainly to be preferred for solo performances, while for the continuo instrument for the concertos and the chamber music the piano should be rigorously ruled out in every case. Purists will no doubt choose organ works by Bach played on instruments approximating to those he knew himself, but there some latitude may reasonably be allowed, so long as the style of performance does no violence to the music. With well-chosen registration Bach can as easily be suitably played on a modern organ as he can be ruined by a performer whose only concern is to have an exciting game with the stops.

# Index

PRINTED IN GREAT BRITAIN
AT THE UNIVERSITY PRESS, OXFORD
BY VIVIAN RIDLER
PRINTER TO THE UNIVERSITY